CHANGIN'
YOUR GAME
PLAN

How I used incarceration as a stepping stone for success

By: Randy Kearse

30 Days on the Wake Up

You would think after spending the last 13 years, 5 months and 2 days in prison, the last 30 days before I was released would be like a walk in the park. Think again. The last 30 days were just as hard and just as long as the mountain of days, months and years that came and went before this point. The last 30 days are somewhat harder in a sense... the slow building anticipation, the lingering questions, the doubts, the hopes, the dreams, the reflections... The long years of loneliness and suppressed feelings all come bubbling to the surface and make for a recipe of uncertainty. While projecting an air of confidence to your fellow incarcerated peers, deep down inside you try not to vomit up the swarm of butterflies swirling around in your stomach. I guess the scariest days of my prison experience were the first few days you arrive and the last few days you're there.

You can't keep your mind from wandering; fantasies of being free, and your reality of still being in prison are like a conflict of interest. Up until the day you're actually IN the receiving room getting processed out, you're still in prison. You have to constantly remind yourself there are people around you who are NEVER EVER EVER going home and there are some individuals who might not wanna see you leave just yet.

Trouble can come like a thief in the night and snatch your release date right from up under you. I have seen it happen. One guy about to go home, another guy angry and bitter at the world, jealous that it's not him leaving, starts a argument with the guy leaving, the argument leads to a fight, stabbing or even worse a killing. Seen guys jeopardize there release date because they felt they had to protect their reputation and not been seen as weak or a sucker.

3

When I was 30 days on the wake up I didn't broadcast the fact that I was leaving. During the long years of my incarceration I always imagine leaving quietly. My last 30 days I was cautiously quiet about my soon to be departure, all the while extremely optimistic about the future.

Only thing was, I had a old open and pending court case in New York, so even though I was ending my federal sentence there was a good chance I could actually be given a state sentence due to the fact I had absconded on a charge I pled guilty to prior to being arrested by the federal government. So my last 30 days of my federal sentence I was going through a lot, emotionally, no one was aware of. Nonetheless, the worst part of my journey was winding down, I had all that time behind me and what I faced in the state was nowhere as serious as what I just finished so, my release date was bitter sweet. Bitter because I still wasn't totally free but sweet because I had done the time and I was one step closer to freedom.

I had seen the inside of more prisons then I would've cared to, but that's how federal prison is, you spend a few years at this facility, a few years at that facility and your security level drops and you're transferred to another facility. Have disciplinary problems you're shipped to another facility.

I did time in Lewisburg penitentiary, Terre Haute penitentiary, Allenwood penitentiary, Estelle medium, and Fort Dix low. I seen my share of violence, petty squabbles, riots, gang bangers banging, and every other imaginable vile act, betrayal, and scheme from murder to assaults on staffs and here it is 30 days before my release date I had survived it all. That was a cause to celebrate within itself. I seen guys die in prison, catch new charges in prison, disfigured, and lose their minds from the pressure of incarceration. 30 days on the wake up.... 30 days away from showing the world what I was truly made of...

4

Changin' Your Game Plan

This book is for those who are ready to win in the game of my life, for real, this time. It is a checklist, a road map, and an instruction manual to help one begin the process of *"choosing"* freedom from mental and/or physical incarceration. This is a powerful, practical, no-nonsense book written from the heart of a man who has been in the belly of the beast and survived to show you a way out too. Randy Kearse shows you what to do with your time, while you're doing time. He shares tools and tips on how to change your mental and emotional state of mind.

Changin' Your Game Plan is not only for those behind the visible walls of prison, but also for those who are seemingly trapped behind invisible mental walls of self- imposed limitations and repetitive thought patterns that prevent forward movement in life. Randy's legacy of truth will lead you on the path to Changin' Your Game Plan. This book can help the untold millions of people who are currently incarcerated, formerly incarcerated and potentially headed through the doors of the criminal justice system; prison, parole or probation.

The challenges you face are many and complex. But they are not impossible to overcome. Going through the criminal justice system doesn't have to be the end of the road for you; it can be the beginning of a journey to a better yourself and create a positive future. Change ultimately starts with you. Randy Kearse is proof positive that you can take a negative situation and turn it into a positive opportunity.

Amazon.com Book Review 2012

Sailing

I got to get my Ship Right... Start SAILING up stream far away from those who refuse to dream.

TIME to SAIL forward and beyond YESTERDAY.

I got to fix this Ship from Top to Bottom because the WATERS of LIFE have WRECKED many of my UNPREPARED SHIPS BEFORE.

Kept them in the dark and in the docks of procrastination while SAILING in circles...

I got to get my Ship Right... Saw too many Shipwrecks that didn't have to be, didn't have to float in the Dead Sea of Drugs and Other Deadly Vices.

Saw too many Ships float endlessly and aimlessly without emotions or drive, without concern or care fueling their journey.

I saw too many Ships SINK in the Waters of stubbornness, unhappiness, no faith, no goals...

I got to get My Ship Right... Fulfill GOD'S purpose, satisfy my own self-worth, TEACH my people, REACH my people.

I got to follow MY OWN HEART, MY OWN MIND and TRUST that GOD IS ORDERING MY STEPS!

I am SAILING on the RIVER BANKS of LIFE being fueled by the SACRED BLOOD of ANCESTORS whose stories MUST BE TOLD WHOLE!!!

I got to get My Ship Right and steer myself to the Shores of Tranquility.

How is YOUR SHIP DOING?
What kind of waters YOU SAILING IN?

Table of Contents

August 2015 will be ten years since I walked out prison with nothing more than two manuscripts, a plan and a strong determination to never return. In the past ten years I've had many ups and quite a few downs, made extraordinary strides and experienced more setbacks than I care to remember. I never gave up or put myself in a situation that could send me back to prison. Tens years filled with challenges, obstacles and adversities, I stayed the course because the time I spent in prison is a constant reminder, no matter how tough it gets out here, it can be a lot worse if I slip up out here. I sent the entire ten year on supervised release. Every day of the last ten years I was one bad decision from returning back to prison.

As I prepare to celebrate my tenth year of freedom, I decided to release a 10th Year Edition of Changin' Your Game Plan. I'm not even going to front, a lot of the same jewels I gave up in the original editions of this book are still relevant today, but there is a lot more to this journey of change I can give you as you stand at the crossroad of your life. This book is my way of reaching back.

I first published Changin' Your Game plan in 2007. Since, I have sold over 75,000 copies mostly hand-to-hand on the streets of New York City, Baltimore, Virginia and New Jersey. I'm a sort after motivational speaker for At Risk Youth, Prison Reentry Reform and more. I have written 4 more books, and actually created the Changin' Your Game Plan prison reentry program. I'm the executive producer of the film series Beyond

Prison Probation & Parole. I'm also the director producer of a film documentary titled, When The Smoke Cleared.

I host Straight Talk w/Randy Kearse a television talk show in Brooklyn, NY. My story has appeared in many newspapers, magazines, on local and national radio and TV. The things I have accomplished didn't happen by chance. They happened as the result of the planning I did while I was incarcerated. I never forget the days, weeks and months that added up to the years I spent behind the stone wall and cold steel barbwire fences of the prison industrial complex. It took me a while to understand, in order to free myself from physical incarceration I had to first free myself from mental incarceration..

This book successfully maps a way out of the negative mindsets and negative behavioral patterns, which keep so many people physically, mentally and emotionally imprisoned. It is my hope that the lessons I have learned on my journey of change will help motivate you to look at your own life and the choices you have made. Read this book with a clean heart and open heart.

Changing your thinking, behaviors and attitudes are part of the process to creating a new game plan. By changing your game plan you will greatly increase your chances of not only successfully transitioning back to society, but also increase your chances of staying out or prison.

By taking the necessary steps to change you gain the power to create a positive game plan for your life. You don't have to wait until you are physically free to take control of your life, because once you make the decision to change you begin taking back control of your life.

Author Background

Born: December 17, 1964 (9lbs 10 oz.), Brooklyn Hospital

Parents: Beverly and Allan Kearse

Siblings: Tracy, Francine, Dennis (DK), Sethpen, Lonnie, Jamal

Raised: Brooklyn, NY (Farragut Houses)

School: P.S. 170, McKinley JHS, Fort Hamilton H.S (Expelled) Eastern District H.S. (a.k.a. E.D. a.k.a. EducatedDummies) dropped out. An above average student throughout school Randy became bored with school. He ditches the books for the working world. (Acquired GED without studying or taking classes to prepare).

First Job: age 17 Minute Men Messenger Service.

First Arrest: April 1982 (For attempted murder which resulted in his first trip to Rikers Island (Adjudicated youthful offender)

First prison sentence: September 1984 (4 months and 6 months probation) Upon his release Randy tried to stay out of trouble, his Uncle Coleman secured him a good job in the garment district and things were looking promising.

Fathered first child: Age 20 (young and irresponsible).

1986 – Walking the tight rope of doing the right thing and running the streets, Randy would eventually get caught up in the whirl wind of the crack epidemic. The lure of making fast money would make him jump head first into the grimy bowels of the illegal drug trade.

Using his book smarts and his street sense he would rise to the higher ranks of known drug dealers from Brooklyn. With his partners in crime (names better left out) they hustled their way from the mean streets of Brooklyn to the too sweet and ripe state of North Carolina. At the height of his hustle, Randy and his team were 25 deep and spread across three cities.

1992 – After a long 6 year run, like the song says, *"When you dance to the music – you have to pay to the piper."* Randy was wanted in the same three cities he once flooded with mayhem and chaos. The Feds, the DEA, the New York City and the Raleigh Police were looking for and gunning to bring him and his cohorts in to dance that last dance. They say it's not over until the fat lady sings, well the fat lady was waiting in the wings for the day Randy was brought before her.

April 1992 – Randy was captured in Chapel Hill NC October 1992 - Randy received 15 years in Greensboro NC November 1992 – The Prison Journey began.....

August 10, 2005 – Randy was released after serving 13 years, 6 months and 2 days in Federal Prison. A changed man with a new game plan....

About The Author

When BET was casting for the show 'The Ultimate Hustler', due to his incarceration, Randy was unable to make the casting call. If there were ever a role for a reality show he was primed for, it would've been 'The Ultimate Hustler'. He would've shown the world the true essence of hustlin', which is, making something out of completely nothing. Taking something negative and turning it into something positive. Randy Kearse is the epitome of 'The Ultimate Hustler'.

Upon completing thirteen and a half years on a fifteen-year federal prison sentence, Randy returned home with a focused determination and strong will to succeed. During the long years of his incarceration, Randy knew he had to change his game plan in order to make it in society. Instead of planning and dreaming of his next street scheme, he worked on reinventing himself.

Part of his makeover included finding a passion for writing, he picked up a pen and began to write. The first of three projects was titled, **STREET TALK: *Da Official Guide to Hip-Hop & Urban Slanguage*** - A 700+ page dictionary/guide which interpreted the whole hip-hop and urban 'street' slang vernacular.

His next project was titled, **Changin' Your Game Plan: How I used Incarceration as a stepping stone for SUCCESS**, a motivational book for his incarcerated brothers and sisters. With **Changin' Your Game Plan,** Randy hopes to encourage and motivate people to do something positive with their time (whether in prison or on the streets) in order to live a better life.

Randy Kearse went into the Federal Prison system Feb 1992 and exited August 2005. As soon as he was released he went to work unleashing his master plan. Two weeks after his release he got a messenger job.... For a few reasons: to put a couple of dollars in his pockets, let his parole officer know he meant business and as a reason to travel around the city promoting his soon-to-be released self-published book **Street Talk**.

In the first ten days of delivering messages he handed out 10,000 flyers for **Street Talk**. He was able to finesse his way into the taping of the VH1 Hip-Hop Honors. He met reporters and celebrities, met rappers and other people while walking the streets of New York. He landed a college radio interview at WSOU 89.8, and did over the phone interview with an Indiana radio station. His book would receive book reviews in online magazines, newspapers and numerous people in the media would request review copies from the publishing company.

A major accomplishment would be the TV interview he did with Tyear Middleton the host and producer of tyeartv.com which aired on the Brooklyn Public Access station BCAT. What would signal Randy's positive comeback would be getting one of the oldest independent publishing companies in the country to buy the rights to **Street Talk**.

While on his daily grind promoting **Street Talk** he attended the Small Press Book Fair on Dec 3. Unable to afford a booth he just rolled up in the place *'hood style*, a handful of flyers in one hand and a copy of the book in the other. Randy wasn't there 20 minutes before he was offered a traditional book publishing deal for **Street Talk** by one of the three leading independent publishing companies in the United States, Barricade Books Inc. Randy accomplished all of these things within the first 90 days of his release from incarceration.

From The Author

Had anyone told me back in the days that I'd travel some of the roads I've traveled so far in this life, I would've told them they were crazy. I doubt if anyone growing up aspires to be a criminal. I was like many of you growing up with dreams. My dream was to be a teacher; follow in the footsteps of my mother. I was an above average student all through school, but became bored in high school and felt there was nothing else I needed to learn. Cutting class, playing hooky, and running behind the girls was more fun (sound familiar?). I'd skip school days at a time, until I eventually stopped going altogether (sound familiar?). Outta five brothers and one sister I was the only one who didn't graduate from high school.

When my moms realized she couldn't force me to go to school, she allowed me to stop going on two conditions: 1. I had to get a job. 2. I had to get my GED (which she arranged for me to take, and I passed easily, without even studying). Dropping out of school was the first of a long list of bad decisions I've made in my life, choices that I regret to this day. I thought hanging out with the so-called cool crowd was the thing. Not realizing that the cool people were really the ones going to school every day getting their education.

My mother tried her best to give her kids the tools they would need out in the world. She emphasized education, working hard and staying out of trouble. Though my pops lived in the crib with us, he was often distant. It was as if we grew up without him. Moms was the one who tried to school us on what to expect out there in the streets. No matter who many times someone tells you something, sometimes you have to learn the hard way in order to understand what they're telling you.

From 16 to 21 yrs. old, I walked a fine line between doing the right thing and getting into trouble. I worked every day and I did my share of dirt too. I caught a 4 month prison sentence during that period for stabbing a guy at a skating rink. The stabbing was the result of a long running beef I had with some guys from Queens. When I came home from doing the 4 months, I went right back to working (my uncle Coleman saw to it that I got my job back). At a time when a lot of my friends were catching cases (for robbery) and going up state, I continued to walk that fine line between right and wrong (freedom and jail).

It wouldn't be until the mid eighties when I'd forget about doing the right thing and completely go the wrong route. It was in the very early days of, what would later be called the 'crack epidemic', that I jumped head first into the vile world of the drug trade. If you didn't know me or the way I was raised, you would have thought I was raised to be nothing more than the drug dealer I had become.

The so-called *game* became my life, the only thing I lived to do. I traded in my childhood dreams, for the dream of being a successful drug lord. I traded in my friends who lived the straight and narrow, for the grimy, untrustworthy, and shady characters you run with in the streets. For the love of the money I became enemies with childhood friends and forged alliances with people I had little or no history with.

In five years, I went from standing on the corner hustling for myself to being one half of a drug network that reached from New York to North Carolina. Me and my partner in crime (may he rest in peace) reached the highest ranks of ghetto super-stardom. We made and spent money like there was no tomorrow. You couldn't tell us we hadn't made it. The future for us was, waiting for the next time to split our illegal profits and re-up with the next drug shipment. To us our plan was flawless. We had been getting away for so long, getting caught only happened to the other people.

The higher you climb the criminal ladder in the streets, the farther you fall. When everything began to come crashing down around

16

me, life began to feel like the feeling you get when you're gasping for air in the midst of drowning. I had already done too much dirt to walk away, so I continued to play the so-called *game* to my last breath.

All the years I had refused to consider the serious consequences of my actions, made the inevitable feel like I had been hit in the head with a ton of bricks. It was no longer dismissing thoughts of what might happen *if* I got caught, now there was a sense of dread of what was gonna happen *when* I got caught. The only thing I was living for now was, staying one step ahead of being arrested. I was on the run. My reign as a ghetto celebrity/drug dealer ended like a scene from a low budget, bootlegged movie. The Big Willie who had once stayed in five star hotels and ate at five star restaurants was now hiding out in a roach infested welfare hotel (the one that doesn't have a phone in the room and you have to wear flip flops in the shower).

The police were tipped off that me and my partner in crime were staying in a hotel in Chapel Hill NC. We were also tipped off that the police were on their way to the room. It was now a race against time. By the time we put together a plan for escape, the police already had the hotel surrounded. By sheer luck, my partner in crime was able to escape and I was captured.

For the next few months I was shuttled back and forth between Federal court and NC state court to face the charges that were pending against me. Knowing I was pretty much in a no win situation, I plead guilty in Federal court to drug conspiracy charges and the charges in state court were dismissed. I received 15 years in Federal Prison.

When I first received my lengthy prison sentence from the Federal Government I remember thinking that I was through, that life was over for me. There was no way that I could conceive of accomplishing *anything* at that point in my life. I felt that I had hit the lowest low of my life. The future??? I honestly felt that I didn't have one. I was like a lot of other brothers around me, just going through the days without any sense of doing something positive. We were men drifting through time simply existing.

Over time I began to take a real hard and honest look at my situation, my life and myself. Slowly I started to realize that life wasn't over for me. In fact, life was just beginning again if I was willing to roll with making some serious and necessary changes. I began to look at my incarceration as a challenge. Did I have what it would take for me to reinvent myself, to make something positive come out of this negative situation? Could I do away with my old self- destructive thinking process and reckless behavior? Could I become a person that would garner respect among his peers and become a son that a mother could be proud of? These were some of questions that I asked myself, the challenges that I set for myself.

With time and a whole lot of determination I set down the path of change and with change came growth, and with growth came a whole new outlook on life. A new clear sense of what was important in life and the ability to appreciate what life really had to offer came to light. While guys around me were still glorifying their misdeeds, reputations, and reckless lifestyles I was looking ahead. Instead of spending time talking about who I used to be, I concentrated on who I wanted to be and who I was striving to become. One of the first things I decided to do was let go of the past. My past had no room in the future.

It wasn't easy. Anyone who is doing time or has done time knows the struggles that go on in prison. I refused to let anything or anyone knock me off the course that I now set for myself. From my many years of incarceration I hope to impress upon you some of the lessons I've learned that lead me to do a positive and productive bid. One filled with growth, maturity, and a new found sense of peace. Doing time isn't easy, but how you choose to do your time will determine what kind of future lies ahead of you.

Too many times I observed brothers doing nothing with their time and it was sad to have witnessed such hopelessness when it didn't have to be that way. We all know the prison system no longer emphasizes rehabilitation. Due to all the budget cuts, programs that were designed to give a person some skill or trade while incarcerated are all but non-existent. Without those programs its urgent we take our future into our own hands. In this day and age of doing time, the only hope an individual has to make it in society after getting out is to take their rehabilitation in to their own hands. If you don't, chances are you're gonna find yourself going back and forth to prison. That's reality.

If you ask anyone who has been to prison and has managed to stay out of prison, how he/she stayed out and the answer will always be, "you have to change your game plan." They made the decision to do something different with themselves. They decided to make positive changes while incarcerated and followed through with those positive changes when they got out.

I know I did. I stop caring how or what people thought or said about me. Yeah I'll be soft but you know what? I'd rather be soft and free then a locked up gangsta or an incarcerated Scarface. I love being free and I've decided never to take my freedom for granted ever again.

Unless you're a Martha Stewart, a Lil Kim or even a Mike Tyson, the chances that you're going to leave prison financially secure or able to live the glamorous life when you're released is slim to none. You don't have the luxury to sit back during your incarceration because you're not financially secure. Many of us don't even have a definite place to stay when released.

If you want to and expect to succeed out here in the free world you have to change your game plan. The game plan you've used thus far doesn't work. Your current game plan doesn't get you anywhere but in trouble.

If you continue to use the same game plan that sent you to prison, then you can only expect to return to prison. It's simple as that. No matter how many different spins you put on a negative game plan, you will only get the same negative results. *There's no right way to do wrong.*

I've been where you are. I've done what a lot of you have done and worse. I used my time wisely. I changed my game plan and now I'm out here doing my thing. Believe me when I tell you, if I can do it you can too. It's all about CHANGIN' YOUR GAME PLAN!

Contributing Authors

At the end of book you will be treated to three stories of change from three brothers who have contributed their personal thoughts, experiences and journeys to **Changin' Your Game Plan.** I had the pleasure to meet two of these brothers, *J.M. Benjamin and Storm Weeks* during the course of my incarceration. The third Brother, *Terence Jeffrie*s I had known briefly prior to my incarceration. All of these brothers have demonstrated tremendous change over the course of their incarceration. On many occasions we'd sit and kick it or walk the prison yard talking about life. Not so much about our former lives, but the life we strive to live, not only while incarcerated but when we returned home. It's during these types of deep conversations you come to realize, a lot of people really want to change but they don't have the proper tools, resources or courage to change. After having one of our long conversations which we'd sometimes brainstorm for hours, I was always assured to walk away with some new thought, perception or idea.

I asked these brothers to contribute a chapter for this book as a way to give recognition to their transformation while locked-down. Their input was important because I wanted to show you that there are brothers who are taking their futures seriously and into their own hands.

It's significant that you know that these three brothers were street dudes just like you. They've hustled hard and they've hustled real. Between these three brothers, they have a combined total of 45 years of prison time. Read their stories and hear what they have to say about using time to their advantage.

No matter the road these men have traveled that landed them in prison, they have all risen above their circumstances to greet change and conquer adversity. It is my greatest hope their words will further encourage and inspire you to walk the path of change during your journey of incarceration.

My Biggest Mistake

Sometimes you have to go back to the beginning to understand how you ended up in a situation.

Looking back, the biggest mistake I ever made on a long list of mistakes was dropping out of school. I was a good student throughout my elementary and junior high school years, but when I got to high school, that's when I lost focus. I started chasing after the girls, wanted to be a part of the cool crowd and was more concerned with making a name for myself in the school, then I was concerned about books and school. As my reputation in school climbed, my grades declined. I started skipping one class, and before you know it I was skipping classes altogether, until I was just going to school to hang out.

With anything in life, when you lose focus; you leave yourself open to all kinds of trouble. I'm not going to blame or contribute my leaving school on "running with the wrong crowd" because I became the wrong crowd.

Many of times and many of years throughout my life I could often see the direct correlation between my dropping out of school and the trouble I would find myself in.

You understand how important education is when you find yourself caught up in the criminal justice system. I know guys who ran the streets, had no real education and when they would get arrested they couldn't read the charges that were being brought against them. They had to totally rely on the lawyer to explain what was going on with them. Nine times out of ten, the lawyer would be a court appointed one, so these guys didn't stand a chance. I seen guys sign plea agreements without being able to fully understand what they were signing.

Preface

Statistics say that 78 percent of the people released from prison will return to prison within 3 years. Why is this? How come so many people after being subjected to such inhumane treatment and degradation return to prison in such a short period of time or return to prison at all? The truth is, most people who are incarcerated fail to prepare for the future. What you have is people going through the motions of time without caring enough to make the necessary changes that'll keep them from returning to prison. During my incarceration, I noticed many brothers doing nothing in terms of preparation for their future beyond prison. Guys would find all kinds of frivolous things to occupy their time with, but very few took the necessary steps to make a change.

Preparation is the one and only thing that can save a person from returning to prison. Without that much needed preparation people wound up going back out to society with the same negative mind frame, destructive behavioral patterns and street schemes they had prior to their incarceration. Without taking the necessary steps to prepare oneself, *'while'* on lock-down, the chances of one being a part of that returnable 78 percent statistic is great.

Changin' Your Game Plan will help put you in control of how you do your time. It will help you gain a whole new perspective on what you can accomplish while on lock- down. Prison can be a stepping stone to a bigger, better, and brighter future or it can be a period of wasted valuable time. No matter how much time you're doing you can walk out of prison with the ability to accomplish great things if you PREPARE!

This book was written for all the brothers and sisters who are currently going through their incarceration aimlessly, with no sense of purpose or direction. For those individuals not making the most and the best of their time, let this book be the motivation you need to start down the road of change. Someone who has been where you are, who has been in and continues to be in the struggle, wrote this blueprint for change. I offer a truthful and humble perspective on how to use your incarceration wisely.

This life-changing guide will challenge you to conceive and achieve positive goals that will equip you for your transition back to society. Getting out of prison is often a daunting and monumental challenge, for anyone, but for those people who fail to prepare for the future, getting out of prison will be like climbing up a mountain barefoot. It's your time use it wisely, squander it and chances are you'll be coming back for another stay.

Keep in mind you're not just preparing to get out of prison, noooo, it's much much deeper then that, you are preparing for your life. Long after you get out of prison you will have to go on with the business of living your life. Everything you do or don't do from this point on to better yourself will have a direct impact on your life way after you leave prison. Getting out of prison is just half the equation, staying out is the other half.

Peace My Brother

I pray when this letter reaches you it'll find you in good health mentally as well as physically. It's been awhile since we last kicked it but nevertheless you've been in my thoughts daily. The last 18 months since my release have moved so fast it's almost as if they passed by in a blur.

After being gone for so long you can kinda forget how fast paced life can be on the outside. I've been on the streets only a few months now but there are times it feels like I never even went away. It's real easy to get so caught up in the day-to-day grind of free life, you don't even have time to think about anything other than what you're doing to maintain out here.

I'm just trying to pace myself and lay the groundwork for all the things I said I was going to do when I got out. It's not easy out here even when you come home with a plan, so I feel sorry for anybody who comes home thinking they can make it without one. A lot has changed out here, A LOT! You can't come out here thinking you gonna play the same street games or run the same street schemes he played back in the days. Forget about hustlin', taking chances and throwing bricks at the penitentiary isn't gonna get it out here no more (not that it got us anywhere before, but dead or the penitentiary anyway).

Coming out of prison you have to have a plan. If you don't one, the chances of you returning to prison are great and you know *these people* ain't playing. They'll lock your butt up for a hun'ned years and not care. A judge will give away a thousand years a week and not lose a bit of sleep over that fact. This is real. Use the prison time you have to make the necessary changes, which will allow you to make a clean break from all this madness.

While I was away I made those much-needed changes. It wasn't always easy, but it was extremely necessary in order for me to make something better out of my life. Most of our lives we live recklessly. We live a lifestyle that promises instant gratification but when all the fast money, the fancy cars and the so-called friends are gone all we have left to show for our life is a gang of years in prison. You can only wonder.... Was it all worth it? I grappled with that question for many years and the truth is, there is nothing more precious than your own freedom. You can't put a price on freedom. The time you spend in prison you can't get back. You can't make that time up. You can only use that time to make yourself a better person.

It's time to *do* something new, not *try* something new. It's time to embrace new thoughts, new ways and new approaches. It's time to set new goals. I'm giving you the blueprint for change and the formula for success, during your incarceration and after getting out.

You don't get to choose how you are going to die, or when. You can only decide how you are going to live, right now. Every day is a new chance to choose. Choose to change your perspective. Choose to flip the switch in your mind from negative to positive. Choose to turn on the light and stop living with insecurity and doubt. Choose to do work that you are proud of. Choose to see the best in yourself, and choose to let go of the past. Choose to truly LIVE, right now.

The Challenge to Change

What is Change? What is the process of change? How do we measure Change? Should we ever stop striving for change? Is change even possible? These are just some of the questions you should ask yourself as you move forward and embark on your journey of change.

Change is the process of becoming different, it's important because it helps us learn who we are, the world we live in and our purpose for living. In order to survive every living thing has to change eventually.

Change isn't always pretty. There are times when change is born out of the worst circumstances. But the underlying bases for change is often the need to better one's situation. Change can bring you face to face with your own personal truth and offers you the opportunity to understand yourself better; how you think, why you think the way you do and how you can begin to think differently. Change challenges you; it will show you things about yourself you may have never taken the time to explore and it will open up a whole world of new opportunities.

Is CHANGE difficult? For a lot of people yes it is. The FEAR of CHANGE is the biggest reason why so many people resist change. People fear a new way of thinking or doing things. They fear not being accepted by family, friends or peers.

The FEAR of leaving ones negative COMFORT ZONE makes many people resistant to change. Inside your negative comfort zone you feel safe, hiding behind your negative thoughts and behaviors. You can do wrong for so long it stops feeling wrong. Many people live in DENIAL of their need to change. Some people want to change but lack the knowhow, tools or information.

How do you get past the FEAR of CHANGE? The first and most important step is to ACKNOWLEDGE there is a need to change. The next step is FACING YOUR FEARS. Once you face your fears you have a chance to explore where your fears stem from, what triggers them and how to manage them.

Change is a process, it's not something will happen overnight. If you embrace change and respect the process of change your chances of making positive changes in your life greatly increase. Each step of this workbook walks you through the process of change. You can judge your success by looking at the gap between where you are, where you used to be and where you want to be. This perspective helps you figure out what remains to be done. You can also judge by looking at the progress you've made from 2-3 years ago or 2 months ago.

How and what we think directly affects our moods. Events or situations do not determine our mood, instead, how we think about the event or situation typically determines our mood. So if thinking affects our feelings, we can change how we feel by changing how we think. Change your thoughts and you literally change the world you are living in.

The Journey to Change

The beginning of your incarceration is a critical time but you won't realize it until later. When I think back, time really started while I was lying up in the county jail going back and forth to court. During this period you haven't been sentenced yet but you're still locked up, so that's part of doing time. We usually don't look at it like that because we're too focused and preoccupied with the outcome of the case itself.

The way one usually starts doing his or her time, is how they'll normally go about serving their sentence. The decisions you make early on when you first get locked up will have a definite impact on where you'll find yourself at the end of your sentence. Decisions like the kind of people you socialize with is extremely important. A lot of times the people you come in contact with in the county jail are the same people you'll see during some course of your incarceration. If you decide to fall in with the click, the homies or run with a gang, the odds are you'll go through your incarceration doing nothing constructive or positive with your time. Birds of a feather flock together. You become the company that you keep. There are positive people in prison and it's those kind of people who you want to socialize with. It doesn't take a lot to see what someone is about when you're locked up. If you do more observing than talking and you can quickly learn what a person is about. Practice and master the art of observation from the beginning of your bid, it can keep you out of a lot of unnecessary drama.

Observing people as well as your surroundings teaches you how to keep people at a distance. You're supposed to choose the people you deal with, not let people choose you. If you can set the pace of how you plan to do your time from the beginning, then you're taking the first baby steps to making a change for yourself.

A lot of times dudes get sucked into this whole *"prison mentality"* thing when they first get locked up. They allow themselves to be brainwashed into thinking you have to act or handle yourself a certain way because you're locked down. This *"prison mentality"* does nothing more then promote negativity. If you do your time in accordance with this *"prison mentality"* doctrine, you'll adopt and live by the so-called prison codes. It's these un-written rules and codes of conduct that keep a lot of brothers stagnate the whole time they're incarcerated. Too many times guys are influenced by their surroundings to the point that they *become* a part of the same surroundings. If you can think for yourself, look around and observe how many people you see trying to do something to better themselves and how many people are just going through time with no real purpose or goal. You have to make a decision about which of the two groups do you wanna belong. The group who is bettering themselves or the group who is not.

Even in the county jail you can make up your mind to do something positive with your time, your time is your life. If you make these positive types of decisions from the time you're first locked up, then if you do have to go to prison, you'll go with the mind set that you're not going to waste your time. Making the conscious decision to make positive changes in your life when you first get locked up, puts you on the right track for change early.

Playing The (so-called) Game

I used to think the life I was living on the streets was part of some kind of "Game". I was *True To The Game,* I was *Game Tight,* I had *Game*, and I *Played The Game* to the fullest. I believed violence came with *the game,* going to prison was just *part of the game,* and death was supposed to be *charged to the game.*

This was the mindset I accepted the first time I was *introduced to the game.* At 14 years old I got *schooled to the game* by my much older uncle Bugs. Bugs literally taught my friends and me *how the game was supposed to be played.* He'd tell us all kinds of slick stuff *like game is meant to be sold – not to be told.* He told us and taught all sorts of illegal cons and hustles. He flashed wads of money and made sure he shared his wealth with us; at 14 years old a hundred dollars meant you were rich.

"The workingman is a sucker", Bugs would say. "I don't want nothing old, but a bankroll" was his favorite line. He wore the finest clothes had the prettiest women and was treated like a celebrity in the neighborhood. Who wouldn't want to be like Bugs? *The Game* was clearly being good to him. By the time I reached 20 I convinced myself I was *in the game.*

At 20 years I was *knee deep in the game.* I thought I had all angles covered like my Uncle Bugs had taught me. You couldn't tell me I wasn't born for this lifestyle. I went to jail a few times, lost a few friends along the way, seen friends go away for *forever.* Seen families destroyed, dreams crushed and innocent people caught in the crossfire of violence, drugs and chaos. My Uncle never taught me about the flipside of the game. As I got older I realized there was a lot of things Bugs left out about the so-called *game.* But that wasn't until I been through enough to see the so-called game for what it really was; a bunch of bullshhh.

The Game is this fictitious way of living that is nothing more than an illusion, which allows people to justify, rationalize and celebrate wrong. It allows those who play the so-called game to go through life without owning up to the destruction and damage they are doing to themselves and others to acquire the rewards the so-called game promises to it's players.

The truth of the matter is, there is no such thing as "The Game". What we call the so-called *game* is actually life itself and life is not a game. If you continue to approach life and the decisions you make in this life as some sort of game there's only two ways the so-called game ends; prison or death.

No one is born to play the so-called *game*. We are taught to adopt the mindset and behaviors that are associated with the so-called *game*. Not everyone gravitates to the so- called game, that's why I don't buy this whole notion people are "Products of their Environment", it's my strong belief people are the "Products of their choices."

Everyone you grew up with did not go to jail/prison, sell/do drugs, carry guns, commit crime, try to solve problems with violence, or didn't become a teen parent, all the negative behaviors often associated to growing up in a particular environment.

The sooner you understand this is not a game, the sooner you can make the changes that will alter the direction of your life. Games are supposed to fun. Where's the fun in spending x- amount of years in prison? Subjecting yourself to pain, loneliness and despair. Where is the fun in watching your children grow up in pictures? Where's the fun in being taken away from family, friends and community?

Self Evaluation/Improvement

There comes a time in everyone's life when they know they're not living right. This is the time when you have to check yourself and that's what self-evaluation is about. Asking yourself the hard questions, the questions that only you know the answers to. Like do you really wanna keep coming back and forth to prison? Are you tired of living the way you do? Are you happy with your life up to this point? Do you wanna grow old in prison?

In prison, just like the streets, the majority of us always look at and talk about what everyone else is doing wrong instead of looking at ourselves and trying to fix what's wrong with us. It's hard to *"self- check"* ourselves because of what we're afraid we'll see. We're too afraid of what we'll eventually have to admit to ourselves. That is, there are so many things about us which need changing, badly. The same critical methods we use to analyze others we need to apply to ourselves. Being able to do this will be a major step toward self-improvement. It's not going to be easy to put yourself under the magnifying glass and admit your wrongs or shortcomings. Not everyone can admit, let alone face himself or herself when it comes to being self- evaluated. You can lie to everyone you know, but you can't lie to yourself and God. It takes time, honesty and discipline to develop the courage and will to change the things one sees about themselves that need changing.

When you take on the challenge to improve yourself there'll be times you'll struggle to make those improvements. Change doesn't happen overnight. As you close the old doors which stopped you from reaching your full potential in life, new doors of opportunity will open. New ways of thinking will take hold of you and the rewards that await you will be great. For those who can't see the value in improving themselves, it is more than likely they will be a part of that returnable 78 percent statistic.

The perfect time to *self-check* yourself is while you're doing this time.

We've been unconsciously conditioned to always look at someone else's problems, now we have to recondition ourselves to look at our problems the same way. The same way we're quick to point out what someone else is doing wrong, we need to be just as quick to point out our wrong doings.

When you do nothing to improve yourself and the way you think, you basically become stagnate at the same level you came to prison on. Stuck at that same level while the world steadily evolves around you and life with its entire beautitful splendor passes you by. Self improvement is having the ability to cultivate the true potential within you. That means stripping away all the superficial facades and getting down to what you're really made of and the great things that you're capable of achieving. Your seriousness, your truthfulness and your determination to improve yourself will decide how powerful you become.

You have to do self improvement on your own terms because prison is no longer in the practice of offering any real opportunities to rehabilitate. Prisons are now geared towards the punishment part of corrections rather than trying to help people rehabilitate themselves. If you don't take the time to do your own self improvement, the chances of you making any positive changes are slim. Self improvement is the only real way you will come out of prison with the necessary tools to keep you out of prison in the future. Because of budget cuts and politicians, more and more programs designed to promote rehabilitation are being phased out throughout the entire penal system. The ability to teach oneself and improve oneself is a great accomplishment and you'll be proud once you do so.

Think about this as you take the steps to improve yourself. Every great person, every person in position of power and every successful person is always looking for ways to improve themselves, to make them more effective when it comes to achieving their objective. Being able to improve yourself will set you apart from the average person who doesn't have a clue what direction he/she is going. The ability to look at ourselves and take a hard and honest assessment of the things that are wrong with us isn't easy, but at the same time it's very necessary. Only you know your true self. Only you can see the things that other people can't. You know your inner self. To accomplish self improvement you first have to stop caring about what other people think about you. Live for what you think about yourself.

In order to make your self-improvement most effective you have to apply the following methods: *self-examination, self-analysis, and self-confidence.* When you apply the *self examination*, you look at yourself and make a list of all your positives and negatives, strengths and weaknesses. You have to be truthful. When it comes to your positives, you want to look for ways to expand them. Your negatives, you want to look for ways to eliminate them. Your strengths, find ways to benefit from them. Weaknesses, find ways to strengthen them.

When you go in the *self-analysis* phase of self improvement you want to analyze yourself for the purpose of better understanding yourself. You wanna understand the reasons you think the way you do, see things the way you do and do the things that you do. You wanna get to the core of where some of your negatives and/or weaknesses stem from? You wanna analyze the bad decisions you've made in the past and figure out what you could've done better. What you need to do to keep from making the same mistakes and what you need to do to make better decisions?

A lot of time we sabotage ourselves with our own unhealthy thinking. We are and we become literally what we think about ourselves and the behaviors we act out. If you see yourself as being a thug, tough guy, a gang banger, a rebel your character is going to reflect those thoughts.

Healthy thinking is about seeing oneself doing the right things in life. Healthy thinking promotes weighing the consequences of unhealthy impulses, thoughts, and actions. Healthy thinking rejects the street mentality, codes and principles. It's about painting a positive picture of yourself and striving to be that person. You have to start the process of thinking healthy.

The only way to succeed in anything is to have healthy thinking. Use healthy thinking to rise above your circumstances or be crushed by the weight of unhealthy thinking, doubt or the fear of changing.

The method of building one's *self-confidence* is taking all the things you've discovered about yourself through self- examination and self-analysis and use those things to build the confidence one needs to grow and become a better person.

As you apply these methods you'll think of different ways to improve yourself daily. You'll approve your ability to humble yourself, to be patient, to think about your actions and the rewards or consequences those actions might bring. You'll improve your ability to be open minded and stop being so critical of other people. You'll work on your faults and shortcomings. You'll improve your ability to see many things in a whole new perspective.

People are judged by how they deal with their worst moments!

Attitude Adjustment

Your attitude will be a major factor to what types of changes you make while incarcerated. Most people arrive in prison with the wrong attitude from day one. Unless you're totally innocent of what you've been sent to prison for (whether you admit it or not), you're the only one to blame for your situation. A lot of people will get mad for me taking this point of view but it's true. The fact that you were involved in doing something wrong, left you open to being a part of the criminal justice system, no matter how unfair the criminal justice system is.

Once you leave yourself open and exposed to the system, whatever happens to you in the process is of your own making. Nobody said that when you got caught up in the system it was going to be fair. Fair or not, you weren't concerned about fairness when you were out there doing your dirt, so who should you be mad at?

The reason why most people go through their incarceration with a negative and bitter attitude is because they don't wanna accept the blame and then take responsibility for their actions. If you can be honest and take responsibility for your actions, then you can take control of the time you're doing and use it to better yourself. If you go through time in denial that it was your actions that caused the consequences that you're suffering, you'll never get past prison on a positive level. You'll go through your incarceration blaming other people for being locked up, when you should be blaming the only person who is truly responsible for your situation and that person is you. Unless you're 100 percent innocent you only have yourself to blame because you did *something* wrong.

One of the biggest challenges you'll face when trying to change is your attitude. Your everyday attitude towards others, towards your situation and more importantly towards life. The change in your attitude strikes at the core of you becoming a better person. It won't be easy when there'll be so many reasons in prison to keep you with a negative attitude. One of your quests on this journey of change is, learning how to develop a new positive attitude. Before now we never cared or even stopped to consider what effects having a negative attitude had on our life. How far has your negative attitude gotten you? Where has it lead you and what troubles have you had because of it?

In the real world, the world where you have to have a job, where you want to own your own business, and where you have to establish credit people take a real good look at your attitude when deciding whether or not to deal with you. And if these people hold some of the keys that you'll need to succeed, your attitude can be the deciding factor between failure or success. In jail there's always something to piss you off. Not getting mail, visits, the people around you, staff, food, etc., but in the real world, there are just as many things or more that'll piss you off too. If you can't get beyond being pissed off when a situation arises, then you're just as good as failed. It wasn't long after I got out here that my attitude was tested and I had to deal with a trying situation.

When my book STREET TALK first hit the streets, this female from one of those urban street magazines tried to play me out of position but I maintained my cool. When you have a positive attitude not too many things can upset you. A positive attitude allows you to deal with trying situations rationally. While I was locked down this female gave my manz Mustafa the ok for me to put a quote from her and the magazine she worked for in my book. So I was like aiight cool. For some reason when she found out my book was on sale, she tried to take me through all this drama about her not authorizing the quote and how she was going to sue me and some other nonsense. Then she comes at me with this weak extortion game wanting me to pay her 500 dollars to authorize the quote or give her 50 copies of STREET TALK.

When she seen I wasn't about to give her anything she had the audacity to ask me to get down with her publishing company. To eliminate this headache I instructed my publishing company to delete her quote from the book. The book couldn't be sold for a few weeks in order to get this situation straightened out, but I just kept my cool and did what was needed to be done.

Had I had a negative attitude, I would've dealt with the situation from a whole different perspective. From the perspective of someone trying to stop me from doing me. We can no longer approach situations using a street attitude like we did back in the days. When it comes to the real world, the street approach, the gangsta or jail mentality won't get it. Your attitude is very important. Take the right attitude towards life and you'll go far, the wrong attitude and you'll eventually wind up in the same situation you find yourself in now. A lot of us have this thing about people telling us what to do, so we get an attitude. We're fast to get an attitude when someone is telling us something that we can benefit from. The reason why we get an attitude is, we don't like hearing the truth, especially when we're doing something we know is wrong.

Along with changing your attitude, you have to change your demeanor, your thought process, and your perception towards life. SUCCESS IS MORE ABOUT ATTITUDE THAN APTITUDE

Think about your attitude as being your passport to a better life, your meal ticket and your business card. A person cannot embark on a journey of change and not address what role their attitude plays in their life. If you already have a great attitude, that's awesome, I haven't met many people in prison who came in with great attitudes, but after working on themselves, they left prison with a positive attitude.

Believe it or not, changing your attitude can change your life

Bitter and Angry

I've been around brothers who didn't have any family support because they ran the *I've changed* game (while in prison) one time too many on people. When they went back to prison for the second, third, and fourth time people got tired of dealing with them. The thing that's so crazy is, these are the same brothers in prison who are bitter and angry at their people on the streets. How can you be mad at your people for not being there for you, when every time they *were* there for you, you let them down. That doesn't make any sense. Dudes fail to take responsibility for the reasons why family and friend support is lacking.

When someone takes the time to support you while you're in prison, you owe that person. Nothing monetary because you can't put a price on support but you owe them the opportunity to see you do something positive with your life once you get out. People give you their support because somewhere down the line they hope and believe that you'll change.

The truth is, you can't be mad at anyone but yourself if people decide to leave you alone while you're in prison. It was your choices that put you in prison not theirs. You didn't take your family and friends into consideration when you were out there doing your misdeeds. If you had, you would've never done anything that would've caused you to be away from them in the first place. (Some brothers won't feel this but it's the truth). Sometimes it's hard to hear the things that need to be heard, but if you plan to make it out here it's better you hear them now. A lot of brothers often say, *"if I would've known what I know now",* well now you know what you know and there's no excuses.

There's nothing easy about prison. I hated being locked up everyday I was, but I refused to let that hate consume me to the point that I became this bitter and angry person mad at the world. Instead I let that hate drive me to make the necessary changes that would keep me from coming back. I've seen dudes do a bid, go home, come back, finish that bid go home and come back for another bid. That's crazy!! But a lot of times it's because they didn't take the time to change.

With all the challenges that await newly released prisoners in society, when you face these challenges filled with bitterness and anger you're setting yourself up to fail. The first trying situation you're faced with and all that bitterness and anger will come pouring out. You'll explode over the littlest incidents and before you know it you'll be out of control. Your bitterness and anger will consume you to the point that it'll take up most of your energy.

You have to stand on your own feet regardless if you have or if you've lost the support of family and friends. Some people will abandon you from the start, others will fade away with time. You have to continue moving forward. If people care and believe in you enough to support you through this journey, you need to recognize you're definitely blessed. Show those people the support they've invested in you wasn't in vain If you look around and there's no one supporting you through this journey you still have to get through it. Don't let bitterness and anger hinder your growth while in prison. Always look ahead. As long as you have a release date, your day will come. So use your time wisely. No matter how grave your situation might appear, remember there's always someone who has it worse than you. An idle mind is the devil's playground. Look around and observe how many people you see doing nothing with their time. Observe how many people are walking around consumed with bitterness and anger. How many people are constantly blaming others for their situation?

Man up and take responsibility for your actions which subsequently led to your situation. You can make the choice to change in the beginning of your prison journey, come to terms with change in the middle of the journey or in the latter part of your journey. It's all good. But don't fool yourself into thinking, you can wait until you're only months away from going home to start making changes. You're only setting yourself up to being one of those returnable 78 percent who spent their time doing nothing to prepare themselves to stay out of prison. Don't fool yourself; you can't expect to achieve anything positive or substantial if you don't work long and hard at it. When it comes to making serious changes there's no faking it. In the beginning of your journey make a promise and a vow to never come back to prison. Then do everything you can with the time you have to keep that promise. Look around and observe how many elderly people are incarcerated with you. Observe how many people aren't in good health and how they don't get the proper medical attention. Ask yourself, is this how you want to spend the rest of your life.

It doesn't take a rocket scientist to figure out, the same negative thought process yield the same negative results if you don't make a change. If you can accept this commonsense analogy, you have a better chance at coming out of prison with the necessary tools to get you further in life then you ever could have imagined Do something for yourself. Walk away from prison having accomplished some sort of goal and ready to initiate some sort of plan with all the confidence that you won't be coming back.

The big question isn't always what are you gonna do when you get out of prison. The big question is, what are you doing while you're *in* prison. Look at those people who leave prison and come right back, then use them as examples of how *not* to spend your time.

They always come back to prison with all kinds of excuses why they're back. It's never their fault. It's the P.O.'s fault, a girlfriend's fault, their manz fault. The excuses go on and on. The truth is, they failed to prepare for the free world the last time they were in prison. When they return to prison they get comfortable again, and go right back to doing the same things they were doing before they left prison, which is doing absolutely nothing.

Many times these are the same dudes who try to pull other guys into doing time wastefully. Right now you're at a unique crossroad in your life. You can choose the path heading toward a better and more fulfilling life or you can continue down the road of recklessness and self- destruction.

Stressed Out

Being locked up in itself is enough to stress anyone out, but it's how you deal with that stress that will determine whether the stress makes you stronger or breaks you down. Prison and stress are synonymous, they go hand-in- hand. Everyone experiences stress but not everyone knows how to deal with it. I've seen guys come straight off the streets stressin' about their girlfriends, family, friends (who weren't looking out for them), how long they're gonna be away and stressin' about the life they can no longer live.

First and foremost, stressing about *anything* and *anyone* is nothing more than wasted energy. Stressin' over your situation isn't gonna change your situation. Stressin' over someone isn't gonna make that person treat you any different than they're treating you now. While you're walking around stressin' over what someone is or isn't doing for you, they're out there doing what they wanna do regardless of how much stressin' you're doing.

In most instances we bring a great deal of stress on ourselves (but of course we don't wanna admit that). We think we're gonna exert the same kind of influence in someone's life as we did when we were out there. If the relationships you had with people on the streets were real, then they'll be real while you're locked up. If the relationships you had with people weren't real, then as time goes by those relationships will fade away.

I've seen brothers who make time unnecessarily hard on themselves because they lacked the ability to stand on their own. The average person on the streets isn't built to stand by someone doing time, so you can't do your time depending on people. You can free yourself from a lot of stress if you can get used to the fact that, you can't make people stick by you if they don't want to. I've seen what stress can do to brothers. I seen a lot of guys get mentally messed up because they couldn't deal with losing a relationship with a female they had feelings for. It's a bitter pill to swallow sometimes. You have to accept certain things while you're incarcerated, and one of those things is having no control over certain situations. Some people will even start talking to you any kind of way. People will verbally disrespect you because they know you're unable to address their disrespect from prison. You can't let that stress you out that's just part of doing time. People will try to carry you any kind of way when they see you're a little down. Instead of getting stressed out, use those vibes to motivate you to do better.

Recognize that people use prison as an excuse to end a relationship, when the reality is, they were looking for a way out of the relationship all along. While you're walking around the prison mad and stressin' over what someone is or isn't doing on the outside, they might just be glad to be free of you and the relationship they had with you. You can't do time stressing about people on the outside. Let them do them and you concentrate on doing you.

Sometimes being abandoned is a blessing in disguise. It forces you to step up and hold your own. I've seen situations where guys had a couple people looking out for them during the course of their bid and it handicapped them. It made them feel like they didn't need to make any changes. They didn't care. As long as their commissary stayed phat, phone privileges existed, and regular visits continued, they neglected to do anything that would keep them out of prison in the future. Often these were the same dudes who wound up coming back because they had it so good the first and second time around.

Whatever the cause of your stress, remember you're not going through something that others around you haven't gone through or aren't gonna go through. It's about how you channel that stress that's most important. Being able to channel that stress in a positive direction is taking control of your time and your future. Not letting external or internal factors that you have no control over dictate stress levels is a major step towards self-discipline.

The proverbial old timer once told me, *"never let people think they can get the best of you while you're locked down."* It's true, usually we're the cause and blame for our own stress. Is it easy to manage stress? No. Is it necessary to manage stress? Yes. You can't do a positive and constructive bid when you spend a lot of time stressed out. You can't even stress over the amount of time you're doing.

Counting the time as it goes by can really stress you out. Let time pass as it will. You concentrate on getting yourself together as the time passes. The more time you spend fixing yourself, the greater the change you'll be able to accomplish. There'll be times when it won't even feel like you're locked up although you're physically in bondage. Your mind will advance and begin to paint pictures of a better future.

A major cause of stress for some people is their inability to let go of their former lifestyle.

Prison is a stressful situation (no doubt). Yet you can't let that stress hinder your growth. I had my share of stress but as time moved on, I learned how to deal with stress. Prison prepares you how to deal with any kind of stress with patience and maturity.

If you can deal with the stress in prison, then you'll be able to deal with stress when you get back in society. That's where you'll have to make your way honestly, get a job and possibly have to deal with people hating on you while you're executing your plan.

Let prison become you're spring board for dealing with stress. If you go through time stressin' it'll be hard to make any kind of significant changes in your life. Often what happens is, the stress turns into bitterness and anger. I've seen dudes get into all kind of situations with other prisoners because they didn't know how to deal with the stress they were going through.

There are short term diversions you can use to alleviate stress such as exercise, reading, playing sports or playing cards as well as participating in recreational activities coordinated by the recreational department. Keep in mind though, these short term diversions from stress can be a good thing and a bad thing. A good thing because everyone needs some sort of outlet for stress, without one, people tend to let the stress build up inside them until one day it explodes. These diversions become a bad problem when you spend most of your time doing recreational activities.

Though these things help to alleviate stress, they don't do anything to build you up with the exception of playing chess or scrabble. Chess helps build your ability to think strategically if you can apply the concepts of the chess game to living your life. Scrabble helps build your vocabulary, again, if you incorporate that into your everyday living that's a good thing.

A lot of brothers like to read urban street fiction to escape stress and block out the outside. Strictly reading this type of material doesn't help you get away from that *street mentality* we really need to be doing away with. Reading is cool, but what you read is extremely important. If a dude only reads books that glorify the lifestyle that brought him to prison and he wants a change from that life, then reading about his former way of living can be counterproductive.

Overall, it's cool to use short term diversions to alleviate stress but for the long term you have to build up enough strength and confidence in yourself to rid yourself of the situations, and people (no matter who they are) who bring stress knocking at your door. Once I accepted the fact that I couldn't control the things that were going on in the outside world, I started putting my energy into the things that I did have control over like me and my future.

Some of the things I did was go to the educational department and see what kind of programs were available to me. I also found a job inside the prison that I could pick up some kind of knowledge. I'm good with my hands so I got a job in the HVAC department where I could learn how to repair air-conditioners, refrigeration units, and things like that. I also picked up some tips in electrical application and wiring. The purpose of these two steps was to structure my days with positive things to do. Things that educated and kept me busy at the same time. After doing that, I saw where I could fit in some time to exercise in an attempt to stay physically fit and healthy.

Knowing that there would be stress periods during my incarceration I wanted to have the upper hand when dealing with those times. To get organized, I wrote down all my ideas, goals and the changes I wanted to make for myself. Then I made a comparison list of what was available to me within the prison walls. I realized, you have to work at pulling something positive out of something negative and everyday you have to work at it. Some people work at it all their lives.

A major factor to consider about stress is, stress can wreck havoc on your health. I seen guys stress so hard they wouldn't eat, sleep, and eventually had to be medicated to help them cope with the stress. You don't wanna be like that. You wanna leave prison mentally and physically sound. If you apply the five "P's" while you're locked up you'll find there is no need to stress about things because you've taken control of your future. The five "P's" are: **Proper Preparation Prevents Poor Performance**. If you prepare yourself properly then your performance in the world will be successful.

Think about this when you find yourself stressing, life is a struggle so why not struggle to do better. If you don't choose to do better and you continue to go the wrong route, when you find yourself back in prison you're gonna be struggling again anyway. Don't claim to be in the struggle if your struggle isn't to better yourself.

Once I got my routine down pat and began the long road of re-inventing myself, I became much more equipped to deal with the stress. Instead of letting the stress work against me I was able to recognize that stress is one of life challenges and it either makes you or it breaks you. This process won't happen overnight But as long as you develop the strength to deal with the stress, stress periods will be far and few in between.

Now that I'm back out here, a lot of the same things I'm talking about are the same things manifesting themselves to me in everyday living. I'm glad I decided to make the changes in my life, especially when it comes to how to deal with stress because it can get stressful real quick out here. Even coming home with a plan you're gonna have your share of stress, so I can only imagine what it'll be like for a dude who doesn't come home with a plan. In the first initial months of getting out you have so much to do and so much going on that sometimes things can get a little overwhelming. I guess when you're not used to doing a lot or being able to do a lot, you find yourself trying to do it all at once.

You'll find and face your fair share of stress out here in society but your prison journey will prepare you to handle it.

Changing Your Perspective

How you perceive your situation will allow you to look past it.

During my incarceration I began to understand that I needed to work on the way I perceived being in prison. What helped change my perception was when I came up with an analogy of how I saw being incarcerated. Going to prison can be like dying; your actions that brought you to prison along with your negative mind-frame, your destructive behavior, and your *street/prison mentality* can be buried while in prison. Going through your incarceration can be like being reborn. Prison becomes a womb. Like an unborn child who pulls nutrients from the mother's womb, you can use the knowledge you obtain in prison as the nutrients you need to be reborn. When the prison journey is close to being over and you've acquired all the things that you need to live a positive and productive life, prison gives birth to the new you.

Once I was able to perceive prison as a situation that can make me a better individual, then doing time became easier to do. The ability to look back at yourself and *see* the changes you've made, the struggles you've had to overcome and your constant struggle to maintain those positive changes will make you feel better about yourself, your life and your future.

Just like the seasons ever changing, your prison journey can be like a life cycle. Changing you for better or for worse and like the seasons, nobody goes to prison and stays the same.

All you have to do is calculate all the things that you've lost as a result of being incarcerated and analyze whether those things were worth losing. What happens is, brothers only look at their incarceration from a one sided perspective, the one side of just being locked up apposed to the perspective of the lessons you can learn while locked up that'll prepare you for the future.

One of the most powerful books that I've ever read is, AS A MAN THINKETH, by James Allen. This books talks about how, what we think, contributes to our successes or failures in life. It says, *"a man is literally what he thinks."* I find that to be true. If you think negative thoughts, your actions and attitude will reflect that negativity. Same way, if you think positive thoughts, your actions and attitude will reflect positiveness. In our thoughts we find ourselves. Often our character is the reflection of our thoughts. Our perceptions are also made up of our thoughts. If we think a situation is hopeless then we won't put forth any effort to better the situation. If we see a situation as being a stepping stone or learning experience then that's how we'll approach it.

The book also talks about when a man changes his thoughts how surprised he'll be at the transformation he'll experience. This is also true. You can't truly change without changing your thoughts. One of the most profound things this book talks about is how, *"Men are anxious to improve their circumstances, but are unwilling to improve themselves."* That's deep.

I recommend reading and studying this book when it comes to gaining a new perspective. Plenty of times I'd reach for this book when I was going through my journey of change. I still read it now from time to time, just to re-affirm that I still have a positive mental discipline and focus that I had when I was away.

Just to add this…. As much as what you *think* is important, what comes outta your mouth is equally important. If you say things like, *I'mma try* to do something, *I'm trying* to do something, then you need to take the word *'try'* out of your vocabulary. When you say stuff like, *I'mma try an' stay out of trouble* or *I'm tryin' to do the right thing* or *I'm tryin' to quit drugs,* it means you don't really believe you can do what you're saying you're *trying* to do. I used to say, *"I'm trying to write a book"* and my friend Stan would say, "Trying??? You're doing it! What do you mean you're trying? Trying is saying you're doing something, but you're not putting forth the effort to get it done because you really feel you can't do it anyway." He'd tell me to stop speaking in the I'm trying sense and speak in the I'm doing sense, because when you speak in the I'm doing sense it speaks in terms of confidence.

Be mindful when you speak in doubtful terms. When you say stuff like, *it's hard out here,* you began to use that as a crutch or excuse. Words and thoughts are powerful tools.

Choices

Returning to society has all kinds of challenges and obstacles waiting for you. All it takes is one poor choice, one choice made without thinking or considering the consequences and that poor choice can cost you dearly. You have to make the right choices even when those choices are unpopular, might cost you friendships or even distance you from family members Making the right choices will be hard sometimes, but necessary in order for you to reach your goals and full potential in life.

As someone who has a criminal history you have to understand exactly how important it is for you to make the right choices. Positive choice and decision making is an important ingredient to your successful transition back to society, your family and community.

A lot of people who make the wrong choices and find themselves in bad situations believe they are the products of their environment, and their environment dictated the bad choices they made, but that is absolutely wrong. You are not the product of your environment; you are the product of your choices.

No matter how bad the circumstances of your home environment (absent father,parents on drugs, physical, emotional or verbal abuse) you don't have to succumb to that, because you do have a choice, even when you think there is none.

Everybody from the hood doesn't go to jail, sell drugs, use drugs, drop out of school, join a gang or indulge in criminal behavior, most people who do so from choice. You might see a lot of negative things going on in your neighborhood environment but that doesn't mean you have to be a part of that. Making the right choices keeps the control of your life in your hands.

Motivation

The same things that might stress someone out can be turned into motivational fuel. The more people gave up on me, the more motivated I became and the more they provided me with motivational fuel. Soon it got to the point that I became obsessed with succeeding, with triumphing over my situation.

Being abandoned can make a person that much more motivated and that much more driven to succeed. That's what we're striving for, to become stronger and wiser. Striving to build our ability to live life from a whole new perspective. You don't need people who doubt you in your new life anyway, so instead of dwelling on being abandoned, focus on reinventing yourself. I guarantee you, when you succeed in making the transformation for the better, you're gonna wonder how you even let yourself get involved with some of these same people you knew from your past. As your perception in life changes you're going to realize that some of these same people never even had your best interest in hand. You're gonna be grateful that they abandoned you, trust me.

The challenge to change motivated me on many days.

On the days it was hard to find motivation I only had to think of all the family members and friends who had passed away and imagine them cheering me on, encouraging me to turn this negative into something positive.

Everything we do in life is motivated by something. When you were out there in the streets you let money motivate you to do wrong. In prison you HAVE to find things that'll motivate you to do right. Staying out of prison was one of the strongest motivating factors for me. As you head down the road of positive change you have to find things that'll drive your motivation.

Another strong motivating factor for me was hearing about other people who've gotten out of prison to become successful, powerful and famous. There's the well known figures such as Don King, Malcolm X, and the actor Roc but there are also a lot of individuals whose stories are untold.

Thoughts of my mother motivated me because one day I wanted her to be proud of me and the things that I accomplish. I wanted to show her that her son didn't waste his time or her time while he was in prison. I wanted her to have a son she could trust and respect in spite of what I'd done in the past. From my own experience, thinking about making your mother proud is a great source of motivation.

Let the dudes who return to prison motivate you too. Look at them and vow to never be like them. Look around you and watch all the dudes who are going through their incarceration aimlessly and let those people motivate you to do something productive with your time. I found motivation in not wanting to repeat the mistakes of my past. Things that motivate you can take you to new levels of understanding and development. Motivation is like gas to keep your determination burning for the goals and changes you're trying to make. Staying motivated keeps you thinking of ways to better yourself, achieve your goals, and reach the type of future you're striving for.

A powerful motivating factor is seeing and believing in the vision you've set for yourself. If you can see it then you can achieve it. You can develop all kinds of mental techniques to cultivate your positive perceptions of life and in turn feed your motivation.

You'll always have people around you who'll hate on you because of the positive changes you're making and they're not doing anything to change. Deep down inside they'll be jealous of you because you're taking your future into your own hands. You can't let these kinds of dudes discourage you from doing what you have to do to move ahead. Instead let their jealousy and hate motivate you to be the best you can be. You'll hear a lot of successful people attribute their motivation to succeed to other people's hate and jealousy toward them.

Learn how to extract motivation from a variety of different sources. Don't let the negative energy from other people steal your desire to do better. Discovering you can motivate yourself in the face of adversity is one of the greatest discoveries one can make about themselves.

Believing you can turn your life around is a great motivating factor.

Life is about choices. Sometimes we make good ones and sometimes we make really bad ones. After the bad choices we always have the opportunity to make better choices. Just because you might have made some bad choices doesn't mean you have to continue making bad choices. Learn from the choices you've made and grow from them. The choice to do better is yours.

Having been incarcerated carries a negative stigma in society but it's not something that you can't overcome. Find motivation in wanting to show society that you have what it takes to come out here and do something positive and productive with your life. I used to say to myself all the time, *"I'mma show these people how you make it happen."*

If you can turn your situation around and better yourself, you'll have accomplished something only a select few people are able to do. You'll be counted among some of the great people who've overcome all kinds of adversity. Once you have bettered yourself and doing things that are positive, people ain't gonna dwell on the fact that you've been to prison. People gonna judge you by what you're doing now, not by what you did in the past.

Anyone interested in personal growth, accomplishing short term, long term and life long goals will have to learn how to motivate themselves in prison. People who are self-motivated are generally more organized, possess great time management skills and tend to have more self-esteem and confidence.

Getting motivated and staying motivated is challenging in prison, especially when you're surrounded by a lot of people who have given up on themselves. I remember how draining it was being in the same room with people who never had anything positive to say. But I never allowed myself to let those kinds of people discourage me. I did my best to stay upbeat and optimistic about the future and the things I was doing to shape it.

One of the things that kept me motivated in prison was believing the reality I was living in would not be the sum of my life. I believed with every fiber of my being I would return to society ready to make my mark on the world. I refused to believe that prison was the end of my story. You had to see me operate in prison, you could not tell me I wasn't going to do some great things when I got out.

Sacrifice and Support

When people do *anything* for you while you're incarcerated, no matter how small that "thing" is, that person is making a sacrifice for you. When you get a visit, your visitor is sacrificing his/her time, travel and visiting expenses. When someone writes you or sends you a package, he/she sacrifices time and postal expenses. And the ultimate sacrifice is when someone sends you his or her hard earned money. People make sacrifices for you to show you they care because no one is obligated to do anything for you while you are in prison.

It's important to acknowledge the sacrifices others have made and/or are making for you while you are incarcerated. Tell people how deeply you appreciate their sacrifices, and how you understand getting a visit, sending a letter, sending money is a sacrifice being made for you.

How can you repay someone who has sacrificed for you during your incarceration? Monetarily you can't, but you can repay someone by showing him or her the sacrifices he/she has made for you were not in vain. You do that by changin' your game plan and doing something positive with your life once you get out.

In order to be successful you have to be willing to give up something. What sacrifices are you willing to make to be successful? You may have to give up your social life, watching tv, certain friends and even sleep in order to achieve your goals. One of the most important things you'll have to give up is your old way of thinking. If you want to achieve success in an area of your life, then you'll have to change what you currently believe about yourself especially if your current belief system is holding you back.

There can be no success without sacrifice. Sacrificing for success means giving up temporary comfort to gain permanent success. A lot people say they want to be successful, but not a lot people are willing to make the sacrifices needed to be successful. Success is simple once you accept how much hard work you have to put into it. Success demands unwavering commitment. It's the dedication you show on a daily basis towards your desired outcomes that will make all the difference in the end.

Playing The Blame Game

On your journey of change you're going to stop at places along the way that will test your will and resolve to change. Some stops are going to be tougher then others and some stops will make you want to throw this workbook in the trash. Some of the things you'll have to face may not make sense at first, but as you let this new way of seeing life, yourself and how the world works around you I promise it will all make sense eventually.

Taking responsibility is one of those places a lot of people will find it hard to get pass. I was one of those people. In the beginning of my 15 year sentence I blamed anything and everybody I could for my situation. I blamed the system, I blamed my emotionally absent father, I blamed the people who cooperated against me, I blamed the judge, the ADA, I blamed the guards and the only person I refused to blame was myself.

I went through my first five years playing the blame game. It wasn't until I started down the path of change that I had to face a real hard truth, that I was the person responsible for my incarceration. All the people I was blaming may have had a tiny role in my situation, but it was me who ultimately created the circumstances in which I found myself. Nobody forced me to sell drugs. Selling drugs involved violence. I didn't run and hide from the violence. I wasn't blaming anyone when I thought I was on top of the world. We place the blame on others so we can deflect the role we played in our own demise.

Once I admitted the truth, that I was the blame, I owned up to that truth and took responsibility for my actions. In that moment I began to take responsibility for my life. Not only for being in prison, being a bad father, hurting my mother, or helping to destroy my community, but all the wrong I had done. I really don't see how a person can change their game plan, without taking responsibility for his/her past, present and future life. Blaming external circumstances for your problems will be a huge obstacle on your journey to improving yourself. There's such a thing as a statute of limitations on the wrongs you feel have happened to you in your life. Once you're old enough to take your life's steering wheel, everything that happens from that point onward is your responsibility. No matter how hard you try to blame others for the events of your life, each event is the result of choices you have made and are making.

Things Changed Out Here

Things are a lot different out here than they were in the mid-eighties and nineties. I'm glad I'm different too. It's like I touched down in another state, I'm a stranger in my own city. There used to be a time when you couldn't go anywhere in NY without running into someone you knew. It's not like that anymore. When you hear people say, *people have moved on*, trust me it's definitely true. Sometimes I find myself scanning faces in a crowd in hopes of spotting a familiar face. When you do run into someone from the past they look so different now. You have to be careful though, you can get nostalgic for familiar faces and familiar places then find yourself going back to your familiar stomping grounds trying to reconnect with people from your past. What will happen sometimes and I'm telling you this from experience, you'll get bored and begin telling yourself you need a little excitement so automatically you'll start thinking about going back around the way. It'll be times like this that you really have to be on top of your *staying and being focus- game*. Keep in mind what a journey back down memory lane can lead to. Old friends, old behaviors and old negative thoughts. You might call yourself going *around the way* for a second, but before you know it you'll be going back on a regular basis.

You see it all the time, brothers come home and call themselves making their rounds around the way, checking for old friends. Everyone greets them with hugs, smiles and laughter. Almost like a celebration. Before you know it, this person's face becomes a constant fixture around the way as if he never went away. By this point, the hugs, smiles and laughter has faded because people who are about something see this brother hasn't changed so they keep him at a distance. People are not going to jeopardize

what their doing for a brother coming home whose actions show he hasn't changed for the better.

There's no one out here anyway, so all the time you're planning to get back up with all your former women or street cohorts, you're wasting your time. Anybody who was somebody who ran the streets back in the days is gone; either dead, in jail or has moved on. Some people just got tired and straightened their life up. You don't even see crack-heads out here like you used to anymore. Remember how you'd see madd crack-heads walking the streets all times of night back in the days? Well it's not like that anymore. *SO YOU KNOW....* if the crack-heads changed their game plan and got their life together we don't have a choice. Some of the same crack-heads from back in the days are now holding down good jobs, raising families, and living their lives. I'm telling you, a lot has changed out here especially in New York.

To show you how much has changed out here, you now have million dollar plus brownstones in parts of Brooklyn that used to be crazy rundown back in the days. I was going to a meeting in Brooklyn and had to take the A train to Clinton and Washington, when I got off the train there was madd white people getting off that stop going home. I was bugging. Mind you, this was the first time I had been back in Brooklyn since the early nineties and I couldn't believe it. Now you know back then white people weren't messing around in that part of Brooklyn. That right there tells you how much has changed out here. When I was doing time I always used to hear dudes say how Giuliani cleaned up New York and now I'm out here I can see the difference. I don't know if it was him or not but I can say this, N.Y. is definitely cleaner compared to how it used to be back in the days.

There's times you may get in your feelings because of the things I'm telling you, but I'm only telling you these things for your own good. Things have changed drastically out here. It's especially going to be rough for brothers like us because of our past. The only way to overcome that disadvantage is coming out here with a plan, the determination to execute that plan and the will to see that plan all the way through. It's not going to be easy all the time but if you have a plan then you start out on the right foot. I remember when I'd call people or when people would write me and say, *'oh, nothing has changed out here'* or *'things are still the same'*. I used to be buggin' because things change daily in the free world. If anything, nothing changes in prison outside of the administration implementing a new policy or something like that.

In the real world things are constantly changing. Stay aware of that fact the whole time you're incarcerated. Never would I allow myself to believe nothing had changed in society.

I believe people say *'nothing has changed out here'* for the lack of not wanting to go into what changes are taking place out here. Then you have those people who nothing has changed for them because they haven't changed. They're still doing the same exact things now, that they were doing before you went away.

Just in the last 5 years alone there have been more changes in the country then at any time in history. If you think these changes don't affect you, you have to be crazy. We're the ones who are first to feel the full brunt of most changes. When the economy is messed up we feel it because prisons start cutting back on money spent on prisoners. We don't even have to talk about the changes in the laws and how they effect us. The deck is too stacked against us for us not to do a change up of our game plan.

Worrying 'Bout the wrong Things

Brothers do a lot of worrying about the wrong things in prison. Instead of worrying about what's going on in the streets or some other frivolous nonsense, bothers should be worrying about what they're doing to prepare for the future. Why would a man who has ten, fifteen or twenty years be worrying about who has his clothes? If anything, he should be worrying about how he's going to acquire new clothes when he gets out. Why worry about who a former girlfriend is dealing with? And you definitely can't go through your time worrying about what the next man is doing, whether he's in prison with you or he's out on the streets.

Too many brothers get caught up worrying about things that hold no significance. Getting your life together and preparing for the future should be the only thing that you worry about.

I never cared what anyone else was doing because I was too busy caring about what I was doing. Whatever a dude did was his business. I didn't care. It's his business and his choice to do whatever he wants to do. If a dude on the streets is gettin' money illegally that's his business. I was never one of those dudes who'd sit around and talk about what I think the next man has or doesn't have when I'm trying to get mine.

Sometimes men gossip more then women do and I used to hate that, seeing grown men get caught up in he-say she- say. The reason for that is, when you get a bunch of dudes together who have nothing positive on their minds you're bound to have some foolishness going on. Put something positive on your mind and you won't have time to indulge in foolishness.

A Mother's Pain

Once I received my sentence my mother told me straight up, *"I'll ride this time out with you, but if you get back out here and get caught up in them streets again don't call me"*, and I can't blame her for that. How much can a mother take seeing her child going back and forth to prison? When you get locked up you take everyone who really cares about you with you. While you're doing time, so are they. Not having your presence around is hard on your family. I could never blame moms for saying that. No mother wants to see her child locked down, then to have that child come home and see him/her go back to prison is especially painful.

While you're doing your time mom is getting older and older and before you know it, you come home and mom isn't that far off from God's calling. I've been with brothers who have lost their mother while on lock-down. I know a guy whose mother died on her way back from visiting him. Many times I prayed that God would give me the chance to make it out to be with my mother. I promised God that if he watched over her that I'd never give her another reason to worry about me. That I would do things that would make her proud of me.

When we out in the streets we don't realize how much the things we do affect our mothers. Especially after they raised us to do the right things in life and we choose to go astray from that teaching. When we do go astray and fail, mothers often take our wrong doing as their failure to be a good mother. But at the end of the day it's always mom who will be there for you.

Moms won't tell you she sent the money order, the package or the letter knowing she didn't. She might not have sent it that exact day because of all the other stuff she's doing and taking care of, but you best believe whatever moms told you she was going to take care of it will be taken care of. When she says she's coming to see you, you can get up the day of the visit knowing that she'll be there. If we owe anyone in this world we owe it to our mothers to do the right thing when we get out this situation. And trust me, the only payback moms wants is to see her baby boy doing the right thing.

Here's something to think about.... When we go to prison we disrupt a natural bond a mother has for her child. For a mother to see her child going through something that she can't fix or help her child out of is painful for a mother. A mother's natural instinct is protect her children and when she can't and has to stand helplessly by and watch her child suffer it tears a mother's heart apart. It was only after I came home from prison that my mother told me how she felt so helpless seeing me in court. Visiting me was especially hard she said, because she couldn't bring me home. Toward the end of every visit she told me how painful it was because she always wanted five more minutes. She said she'd get outside the visiting room and remember something that she wanted to tell me and couldn't.

Our mothers don't deserve this pain. No matter how far we fall, our mothers are always there showing us unconditional love. They continue believing in us even when we stop believing in ourselves. We need to show them something now. We need to show them that we can turn our lives around and make something positive out of ourselves.

Check out this story..... There was this guy, most of his life he was in and out of prison. A few years for this, a few years for that and each time he went to jail he would write his mother and tell her how much he changed. His mother would write to him, send him money and lookout for him every time he went to prison. After doing a few years on a another sentence he got out and went to see his mother promising her he was going to do the right things and basically telling her all the stuff he'd normally tell her while he was in prison and immediately after getting out of prison. Well a few months went by and low and behold he went back to prison. He had been drinking and doing drugs one night and decided to rob a store. Of course he got caught. As soon as he hit the county jail he started writing his mother. Letter after letter he wrote and he never received a response. A couple weeks went by and he still didn't receive a response. It wasn't until he went to court when he found out, that the night of the robbery while he was fleeing in a car he hit and killed someone...... and that someone was his mother.

I talked to your mother today....... She stopped by table while I was on the streets selling copies of my book. The cover of my book caught her attention. She picked up a copy and while she read the back cover I could see the pain on her face and the hurt in her heart. I could've shed tear with her as she started telling me about the weight she carries around with her because of your situation. I could've shed tears with her because she was my mother too. I wanted to shed tears with her when she told me she lost two sons, one buried in the graveyard and the other one buried in prison. I almost shed tears for her when I hugged her. I told her I was her son, a strong black man who refused to give up, lay down or accept defeat..... We talked about 15 – 20 minutes, she did most of the talking and I did most of the listening. She needed an ear of someone who could understand what she was going through.

I pray that you'll be with your mother again when this journey you're on is over and that you'll erase the pain in your mother's heart and replace it with happiness and smiles forevermore.

Don't wait until it's too late for your mother to see you doing something positive. Prepare to make her proud now. You should see the look on my mom's face every time I show her something that's been written about me on the Internet, in a newspaper or when I'm on the radio. She was bugging when I did the TV interviews. She was telling everybody.

After all your mom has been through she needs your changes just as much as you do.

40 years old Running Out of Time

Had I listened to the guys who weren't doing anything positive with their time I would've come home in a worse off position than I was before I went away. There's a big difference when you're out there runnin' the streets at a young age and when you're trying to run the streets at a grownup age. I left the streets for prison at 26 going on 27 years old. I came home at 40. I turned 41 only four months after being on the streets. A man in his forties who doesn't have anything to show for his years on this earth is a sad case.

People will give brothers like us the benefit of the doubt because of the length of time that we've been away, but after that, it's like *'ok now what you gonna do?'* If you don't have a plan for yourself at this age, especially after going through what you've gone through, you're going to find that not too many people really wanna be bothered with you. People out here are too busy trying to get what they're trying to get than to be wasting their time dealing with dudes who have no direction, goals or dreams. When you're 40-45 yrs old and broke, you in trouble. But, if you're 40-45 yrs. old and have something substantial going on that'll bring you financial security you're definitely the man.

For many of us this is basically our last stand. Our last chance to get it right. There's no more excuses after this. No more *'I was young' 'I just did a stretch'*. How many times moms used to tell us *"you get outta life what you put in to life"*? Some dudes never get it. To have done all the things we've done and seen all the things we've seen, it only makes sense that we change the nature of our game plan when the situation looks hopeless. That's the true nature of a hustler, having the ability to make something out of completely nothing. How many times are we tested to make something happen when we're on the streets? How many times did our mere survival depended on being able to come up with some scheme, hustle, or plan that would generate a cash flow. We'd wreck our brains trying to come up with a plan. Not to mention how we'd put ourselves in all kind of harms way and jeopardy day after day just to make some fast cash.

With all the intelligence brothers possess behind the wall, it's a wonder that brothers aren't coming home from prison and taking corporate America by storm. We definitely have the time while lock down to learn how to do various different things. The same way we had to learn how to sell drugs, find connections, rob people is the same way we can learn how to do something legal. That makes sense to me. Plus, being legit is a lot less stressful, a whole lot safer and rewarding. Do you realize how many times we courted death when we were on the streets living wild- style? Going up in drug spots copping weight from anybody who had the good stuff, not caring that we could be walking into a setup or robbery homicide. It's a wonder we never met the same kind of fate that a lot of other brothers met when they were set up for robbery and wound up dead during the course of the robbery. In the streets you never know what to expect and who to expect it from. One time this chick who's a rapper now set me up for a stickup in a hotel. I had to fight for my life in this life or death confrontation all because she seen me as a easy way to make her some quick money.

We get so when we're out there, we never think something like that can happen to us so we become real laxed. If I had let the dude back me down into the hotel room I pretty much might not be here today writing this. It was only a strange turn of events that night that kept me alive. You never know what you'll do when you're faced with a life-death situation. You do what you have to do to survive. In today's world you have to change in order to survive.

You have to learn how to adapt in order to survive. You have to let go of your old ways of thinking in order to survive. We don't have the luxury of youth on our side anymore where people would blame certain behavior on youthful indiscretion. Any misstep at this age will be detrimental. You get hit with a ten or fifteen year sentence in your late thirties or early forties you lessen your chances of being able to bounce back from that sentence.

Down But Not Out

Before I took the fall that sent me away I ran the streets hard. Just like a lot of y'all, I was caught up in my own hype. The fast money, women, cars and the ghetto fame that comes with the so-called game is all I lived for. I ran the streets like I owned them. When my run was over, I went to prison financially broke and emotionally drained. The streets had taken its toll on me. In some ways prison was like rehab for me. A chance to break the addiction I had for "the streets". No matter how far I had fallen in life I knew I was down for a minute but far from out. Even before I really understood the journey I had to embark on I knew I had to do something to turn this situation in my favor.

What really used to get me mad when I was locked down was, seeing so many brothers who walked around with this look of defeat on their faces. A lot of brothers looked like they had lost their swagger. Instead of thinking about how they were going to make their come back, they walked around with this sense of hopelessness. As hard as it was, I stayed away from brothers like this because I didn't want to be infected with the defeated bug. I never accepted defeat in the street so I wasn't about to accept defeat while in prison.

Based on the way I carried it on the streets, I knew if I could make the necessary changes to reinvent myself I could succeed in anything. I wasn't gonna be one of those dudes who claimed he changed and as soon as he gets out, he goes right back to doing the wrong things. People would see the changes in me. Talk is cheap from the jail house. People get tired of hearing all that *I changed* talk they wanna see it. Real change isn't the type of change you talk about, it's the type of change you be about.

Real change is being conscious that everyday you strive to better yourself. You have to live by those changes and you have to believe in those changes.

It's not enough to take a couple classes or a trade course and think that's all you need to change. I've seen guys go to school everyday but still promote and bc involved in all kinds of negativity. That's not the kind of change I'm talking about. To make a sincere effort to change, one must sidestep all the nonsense. Take for instance the dude who reads his bible every day and goes to church but as soon as he hits the streets he throws the bible under the bed, throws the kofi up on the shelf and keeps it movin'. How about the guy who convinces his family and friends that he's changed only to come home and go right back to the street life.

Change is learning new things, learning how to do different things, so you have to try different things. You definitely have to expand your mind. Until you try to expand your mind you'll remain in that limited mind-frame that says going to prison is just part of being in the so-called *game*. Change isn't something you tell people about, it's something that people see. You can tell people all day everyday that you've changed but until they can actually see the changes, it's all talk to them.

The mistakes I've made and the time I've spent in prison don't define me. Those experiences are just part of my life story. We go wrong thinking the time we do makes us who we are, it's what we do with the time while incarcerated that truly make us who we are. Prison can be a stepping stone if you allow yourself the opportunity to grow and change with the time or it can be a weight that holds you down from reaching your true potential.

Staying Sucker Free

While I did my time I did my best to stay sucker free. I didn't let myself get caught up in all the nonsense that was going on in the prison. Dudes can keep a bunch of drama going worse than women do. I stayed out of gossip and he- say she-say. I didn't let dudes bring that type of stuff around me. I respected brothers and brothers respected me. You always gonna have your trouble makers, but for the most part, trouble finds a dude when he puts himself in certain kind of situations. While you're locked down you have to stay sucker free. Suckers will have you in all kinds of nonsense every chance they get. I might be cool with a dude, but as soon as I seen he was into nonsense I'd shake'em like a bad habit. As few brothers as there were, I always tried to associate with the ones who were on the same positive page as me.

I spent a lot time in the library and I found most of the dudes who came to the library had something on their mind or were trying to find something to put on their mind. You wouldn't find too much nonsense jumping off in the library. I used to go to the library to think and to get away from all the craziness surrounding me. It was one of the few places a dude can go to think and I'd go every chance I got. I'd spend so much time at the library, when dudes would see me walking across the compound they would say, *'I see you going to the office'* or *'where you comin' from the office?'*. If you wanted to catch up with me, all you had to do was look for me in the library.

I stayed away from playing basketball or any contact sport because that was a breeding ground for trouble. I seen guys get into all kinds of beefs on the basketball court. I seen guys wind up getting stabbed or stabbing someone over a beef that started on the court.

Sometimes days would pass after an initial incident on the court and the beef would simmer and simmer until it boiled over and blew up. Violence always being the end result. When you go out there on that basketball court you never know what's going to jump off. I've seen dudes who were madd cool with each other fallout in the midst of a heated basketball game.

Disrespectful things get said and before you know it these same two buddies were at war with each other. I never forget the time a dude named Sarge let a dude tell him to *suck his joint* in front of the whole gym. He let the guy disrespect him, but most brothers wouldn't have. To avoid these volatile types of situations I stayed away from them.

If it wasn't the basketball it was the TV. I barely watched TV. If I did it was mostly news or informative kind of shows. I was never into sports so I wasn't missing anything when it came to that. Sports on TV was always a cause for trouble. I've seen a lot of brothers get their head split wide open over the TV. Especially those dudes who thought they came to jail with a TV. You know the ones, always sitting in front of the TV like they're in their living room or something. Then you have the dudes who like to turn the TV when other people are watching it. The worse of all is the dudes who wanna watch BET all day every day. They'll sit there watching the same videos over and over again. It made you wonder if they were trying to live life through the videos. The thing that really killed me was, seeing grown men 35-40 years old and older, watching 106 and Park. I used to just shake my heads in disbelief. Brothers need to get a firm grip on things when they're away before they turn around and be too old to have a life.

Let me give you a few examples of suckers. Suckers don't want you to change so they'll look for any opportunity they can to remind you of how you used to be. Suckers will always talk negatively about everything and everybody. Suckers will drag you into drama they started. Suckers will back-bite and back-stab you first chance they get. Suckers always wanna debate and argue about anything and everything. Suckers have the latest scoop on everybody in the prison. Suckers stay in other people's business.

I've seen too many dudes get jammed up behind a sucker. I seen brothers wind up with more time because a sucker manipulated them into doing something they really didn't want to do. Suckers will instigate and prod two people who may have had a couple heated words between each other, into having a physical confrontation. Suckers wanna be into everything going on in the prison. Suckers try to get their love ones to smuggle drugs into the prison for them.

Here's a couple things suckers will say, *"man I ain't never changin'" "I'm not changin' for nobody", when I get out my kids gotta eat", "I got another bid in me", I know how to do it this time."*

A sucker will read this book and call it nonsense, yet he'll leave prison ill prepared for the future and wind up coming right back.

Staying sucker free is about staying clear of people who bring negative energy, doubt and disbelief into your space. In prison it's not as easy to simply steer clear of suckers as you can on the outside. Suckers in prison like to stir up chaos and confusion by spreading rumors, gossiping and instigating situations. Prison suckers are generally miserable people who are not happy until everyone around them is miserable as well.

Learning how to live sucker free in prison will teach you how to live sucker free on the streets because in prison you are surrounded by potential suckers everywhere you go; on the cellblock, at work detail, the rec yard etc. On the streets you gonna find at least one sucker on your job, in your family, posing as a friend and maybe even masquerading as your significant-other.

Surround yourself with positive and conscious minded people and don't be surprised when you find yourself growing and feeling good about the future. If you allow a sucker to make you react negatively to a situation that jeopardizes your freedom first, and your progress and growth secondly, you will turn out to be a bigger sucker than the sucker who got you tripped up.

Mentally Incarcerated

There are two types of incarceration. The physical kind where you're surrounded by fences, barb wire and prison guards. Then there's mental incarceration, where your mind-set holds you back from achieving anything positive in life. A mind-set that keeps you from wanting to better yourself and/or better your situation.

You don't have to be 'in' prison to be mentally incarcerated. People are walking through life everyday stuck in a mental prison. There are so many different reason for mental incarceration; fear, ignorance, education, negative influences, and family upbringing are just a few of the reasons people become and stay mentally locked down.

My uncle Coleman would say, *"If you knew better you'd do better."* The sad truth is, there are so many people who just don't know any better. You have a large amount of people who are content with having nothing or the little bit that they have. A person who *won't* work can be happy with a pack of cigarettes, a beer and watching television all day. People who think their worth is based on how well they dress will spend their last money trying to look good. Men who have no aspiration, don't care to own a house, own a business, get a degree, travel or experience things they've never experienced.

Mental incarceration is far worse then physical lock down. Worse because most people don't see anything wrong with the way they think when they're mentally incarcerated. It's the kind of mentality that makes someone say a person thinks he/she is white because that person speaks proper English. The kind of mentality that promotes having fun now and never mind about the future. The kind of mentality that sees nothing wrong with being unfaithful in relationships. That kind of mentality that makes people feel they can't catch the HIV virus so they indulge in unprotected sex. That kind of mentality that keeps people from aspiring for a better life.

Though this book was written primarily about the journey of change one has to embark on while locked down, it can be applied to so many people who are doing time on the streets mentally incarcerated. When you're physically locked up you're really at an advantage when it comes to freeing yourself from mental incarceration because doing time gives you a chance to think and hopefully gain a fresh perspective and approach to your way of thinking.

Anytime you can't break free from a mind set that keeps you from moving forward, keeps you in hurtful situations and keeps you from seeing your full potential you're mentally locked down.

It's really sad to see so many people who have no dreams, no aspirations, or no goals in life. People who think all there is to life is what's going on in the 'hood. And it's equally sad to see people I grew up with, still stuck in the streets with nothing to show for their life.

The only way to free yourself from mental incarceration is to change.

Institutionalized

Everyone in prison runs the risk becoming institutionalized to some degree during his or her incarceration. When you have to adapt to and make adjustments in an environment that keeps you on guard 24/7, makes you feel isolated and devoid of emotions or feelings, it can leave an everlasting an impact on your psyche. Making an simple adjustments like walking on one side of the corridor to eating a meal in as little as 6 minutes done over a period of time can become so routine you may forget it was an adjustment you made for survival purposes. The challenge you face is to avoid allowing the adjustments you make to survive your prison experience, from becoming a permanent part of who you are?

Some will say being institutionalized is a state of mind, and on a case by case bases it's according to how an individual process his or her prison experience. One person can leave prison after over a decade and not exhibit any behaviors associated with his or her incarceration, yet someone who may have been in prison a few months may go home with many of the behaviors associated with being incarcerated. Prison changes everyone no matter who it is. No person leaves prison the same as he or she went in. Only you can determine how much of an impact prison will have on you, and whether impact will be a negative or positive one.

The prison environment promotes dependency upon policies, practices and structures over personality, empowerment and free will. Spontaneity and ordinary personal interactions have all but been extracted from the prison environment. Many of the temporary adjustments you make to survive your incarceration are not adjustments you want to bring home with you.

One reason people become institutionalized is, they lose touch with the way life is lived in the world outside. People get so used to the daily routines, the monotony and t "doing time" coping mechanisms they forget they are living in a manufactured environment. Day after day, week after week, month after month, and year after year of "sameness" will erase any traces of real world normality if you let it.

Gettin' Ya Mind Right

When you walk back into the free world, you have to be mentally prepared for the road ahead of you. Even with the best-laid plans, you have to be mentally prepared to follow through with your plans. If you haven't mentally prepared yourself for all the scenarios, distractions and impulses awaiting you when you walk out of prison you're going to be overwhelmed with your newfound freedom to make choices again.

Getting your mind right means mentally preparing for getting out of prison. If you are easily swayed or influenced by the distractions on the streets you won't stand a chance. Distractions come in all shapes, sizes and forms at any given moment.

When you're mentally prepared to leave prison, you already see the big picture. You've incorporated and understand how important being patient is to your success. You are prepared to use the lessons your incarceration has taught you to guide you on the right path in life. You know the stakes are high. You can strengthen your mind through exercise, training and discipline.

Very often we sabotage ourselves with our own unhealthy thinking. How and what we think directly affects our moods. Events or situations do not determine our mood, instead, how we think about the event or situation typically determines our mood. So if thinking affects our feelings, we can change how we feel by changing how we think.

Reading will definitely help you get ya mind right in prison, but it's not how much you read, it's what you read that will determine how reading plays a part in your progress. If all or the majority of your reading consists of books or magazines that promote the same lifestyle you're trying to get away from, the same lifestyle that sent you to prison, the same lifestyle that sent a lot of your love ones to the graveyard, it's going to be hard to get ya mind right, because your mind won't experience growth

You have been mentally poisoned and the only way to get ya mind right is to mentally detoxify from all the poisons that have corroded your mind; the drugs, violence, crime, money, prison, gangs etc. Depending on how long your mind has been poisoned, it might take some time to get your mind right. The first step is cleansing your mind and your life of toxic people and toxic relationships that do not promote positive growth. Change your thoughts and you literally help change the world you are living in.

Just like you have to be careful what you feed ya body, you have to be careful what you feed ya mind. The same holds true to the music you listen to, the TV you watch and the information you take in from the people around you. If all the music you listen to is negative, all the TV you watch is negative and the conversations people are having around you are negative, then you leave yourself little or no room to grow because your mind is still being fed negative information.

Prison Parenting

Being a parent from prison is one of the biggest challenges an incarcerated mother or father can face. Add no cooperation from the child's mother or father and it would seem like being a parent from prison is impossible. The steps you are taking to change your game plan will help you become a better parent upon your release, but how do you approach being a parent now.

Being in prison takes away your parental influences. You won't be able to exert authority or discipline your child from prison effectively. As a parent in prison, your role is to become more advisory then authoritarian, and when you can learn accept this, it will make the parent - child relationship work a lot better for you and your child.

As the cause of this situation, you have to be mindful of what your child is going through and not let your own challenges, frustration and circumstances make the situation about you. Your child is the victim of the decisions you made.

A child might exhibit resentment towards you because you're not a constant presence in his/her life, and that resentment might manifest itself in rebellious behavior, disrespect and/or anger. You have to be patient with your child and allow him/her to work through any issues he/ she has with your absence. Trust is one of the issues, which may impact the relationship with your child. The fear of you returning to prison may make your child hesitant to get close to you emotionally. Trust has to be established.

In cases where there is no or limited communication with your child you can start a letter writing campaign or keep a journal of your thought, hopes and wishes for your child, then you can give it to him/her when you get out. This is a good way to let your child know that in the midst of your worst life's moments you were thinking about him/her.

Your experiences can be the biggest deterrent to your child who statistically will face a lot challenges because of your absence from his/her life. Be prepared to answer your child's questions about your incarceration, openly and honestly.

Leaving A Legacy

What is your legacy going to be? What mark are you going to leave when your life on this earth is over? What will people say about you? What will your tombstone read? What will you be remembered for? Ask yourself this, and be honest, *"if I died today what would my legacy be?"* Would it be all negative; jail, drugs, street schemes, mental incarceration, etc? Would it be half negative-half positive? Would it be all positive? What would your legacy say about the way you treated people; family, friends, kids, siblings? Were you kind to your fellow man/woman?

Take some time and consider these questions. You don't wanna leave this life without leaving something that documents your time here. As you travel your journey of positive change, begin to contemplate what you want your legacy to be. Your legacy can be left in many ways; how you treated your follow man or woman (good or bad). The things you accomplished during your life, the types of assets you accumulated. The struggles you overcame during your time here.

If your legacy up to this point would be all negative, it doesn't have to stay that way. You have the power to change the outcome of your legacy for the better. Don't wait until most of your life has passed you by before you consider what you want your legacy to be. Legacies are built over the course of your life. Your legacy is your testament to your life. From this point forward, start living your life in a way that you'll leave a positive legacy for love ones who will remember you.

Tapping into your Spiritual Side

No matter what your religious beliefs are, we all need to tap into our spiritual side. If you're like me, you're not all that versed in scripture and you don't know about the Koran, but you do know your spirit is in search of peace. The kind of peace you can only find when you begin living right. When you're on the streets living foul, the reason you go through so many trials and tribulations is because your spirit is in constant conflict with the wrong you doing.

Everyone has a spiritual side. Now is the time to tap into it. Just because you don't go to church or you don't quote scripture, doesn't mean you can't develop a personal relationship with the Most High. We have to recognize and give thanks to the Power that is greater than all of us. We couldn't have come as far as we've come without the Higher Power allowing us to.

Every time I wake up in the morning I give thanks, because every day you awake is a blessing. Life isn't guaranteed to anyone and you better give thanks for still having it.

A lot of brothers don't even realize how blessed they are in their present situation. We're all blessed just to be alive. We've lost countless soldiers in this so-called *game*. Some we knew and more who'll forever remain unknown to us. But casualties nonetheless. The brothers who have left before us don't have any more chances to do right. They don't have the opportunity to make better choices. We do. As long as we're alive we have a chance to do better if we want to. The thing is, '*if we want to*'. We've come a long way and we still have a ways to go.

Many of us don't know how to count our blessings. Tapping into your spiritual side allows you to recognize the many blessings you have, the more righteous a man's actions and heart, the greater chance for him to receive blessings.

Prison Saved My Life

Many brothers attribute prison to saving their life because of the reckless lifestyle they were living. Whether dudes are man enough to admit it or not, had it not been for going to prison many dudes would have gone straight to the graveyard. Too many of us would be dead right now if prison didn't take us off the streets. The brothers who realize just how dangerous of a life they were living, will tell anyone that prison saved their life. I know prison saved my life without a doubt. If I hadn't caught the 15 years in the Feds I know I would have been dead or so far out there that I would've ended up with a life sentence. When dudes who I was extremely close too started getting killed, I know for a fact I would've been somewhere in the mix of the drama had I been on the streets. Too many times I called home and mom would tell me one of my dudes got killed. Guys who I was madd cool with, broke bread with, grew up and got money with.

It has to be bitter sweet when your love ones are glad you're in prison rather then on the streets when your friends start dying. It was the losing of close friends and family members that truly made me realize I had a second chance at life. My mother would always say, *"make the rest of your life count for something. Look at all the people you who aren't here anymore. Make your life count for something."*

Even though we catch the long prison sentences, sometimes it can actually turn out to be a life saver. Understanding that, is something that should motivate you to change your life and lifestyle while you still have the opportunity to. When you're laying in your bunk at night trying to make sense of all the things that you've been through, you have to understand that you're still here for a reason, you're still here for some kind of purpose.

Man, there's so much more to life then the negative things we used to do. When you change it's like being born again. I'm doing things I never thought I'd be doing now. A lot of the same things moms used to tell us back in the days are the same things we have to confront now. Well moms do knows best.

Changing for your Kids

It's hard on children when their father is in prison, especially girls. The father is the first male a little girl has a relationship with and if that relationship isn't there little girls have it the hardest. As they grow up girls often seek the love and attention they didn't get from their father from guys they meet in the streets. They go into relationships too young and unprepared to handle their feelings and wind up going through all kind of problems. Those insecurities and self-esteem issues they have manifest in ways that leave them easy targets to be taken advantage of.

Write your children and call them whenever you can. Try to maintain the best communication with them as possible. I'm telling you right now, when you get out, there's going to be issues with them that you'll have to deal with. Straight up! That's why it's imperative that you make the critical changes in your life while you're away. Give them a reason to look at you differently. Give them something to feel good about when they do come around you. Let them see their father didn't waste his time while locked up. This will be one of the greatest gifts you can give your children when you get out. Show them you were able to overcome your situation. Show them a person can change their life around if that person chooses to. You'll be setting a hell of a positive example for them. Making moves that you can include them in will help re-build that bond that's been damaged because of your absence.

You don't wanna be one of those fathers who comes home and his kids don't want nothing to do with him because they think he hasn't changed and eventually wind up going back to prison. Kids who feel that way about their father keep their distance because they don't wanna get hurt. They're hesitant because they see a lot of fathers come home and go right back. Show them by your works and not by your words alone. Show them that you've put that street mentality behind you.

Re-establishing a relationship with your kids won't always be easy, but trust me, if you're doing the right things it will make the re-establishment a lot smoother.

Drugs the #1 Pitfall

Drugs have to be the number one pit fall for brothers when they get back out to society. So many times dudes put getting high in front of their freedom. In prison drugs are sometimes readily available but they're not as readily available and plentiful as the streets. During the course of your incarceration there'll be times you're gonna wanna get high but you'll be unable to get the drugs you need to get high. These are the times you'll be going cold turkey. This is the perfect opportunity you should use to break free from the addiction that causes you to choose drugs over freedom. Most prisons have a drug program for you to get help, so why not take advantage of it? You can't make it out here if you have anything to do with drugs. Whether you use or sell them. There's no such thing as getting high just one time or selling drugs just to get on your feet.

No matter how much you profess to have changed, if you get high or go back to selling drugs you haven't changed. What better time to exorcise those drug demons? What better time to admit you have a drug problem and you need help? Admitting that you have a problem is the first step to taking back control of your life. The user as well as the seller share a form of an addiction. One is addicted to the substance and the other is addicted to the money and the false sense of power he/she holds over people who are addicted to the substance. Both need and feed off of each other.

As someone who sold drugs I wanted to understand and break free from my addiction. I took the drug programs that were offered in the Federal system and it helped me immensely. I didn't care what other guys had to say when they knew I enrolled in the drug programs I did what I did for me and the betterment of myself. And I'm glad I did.

If you have struggled with drugs in the past, now is the time to break free from addiction. Your freedom will very well depend on it. They don't grow enough cocaine, heroin or weed for me to ever think about getting back into drug dealing.

No one time deals, hooking other people up with connects and no trying to make a couple of dollars on the side, NOTHING!

People, Places & Things

People, places & things can keep you out or send you back.

People – Whom you surround yourself with, or just even associate can have a negative or positive impact on your quest to stay out of prison. A simple association with someone who is doing something wrong can jeopardize your freedom. It's unfortunate but you have to keep your distance from anyone who is not living a positive and law- abiding life. You know the terms, *"birds of a feather flock together"*, *"guilty by association"*, *"Show me your friends, and I'll tell you who you are."* You get caught-up in a situation with the wrong people, right or wrong, your history alone can sink you. Put yourself around positive people and your chances of fining yourself in negative situations decreases. Negative people attract negative situations.

Places – There a general rule about places, if you hangout, frequent or find yourself in places where there's a possibility of violence, drug activity or you feel you have to possess a weapon to be safe you are in the wrong place. Very rarely do we go places unaware of the atmosphere or type of people who will be there. Being *"in the wrong places at the wrong time"* is not an excuse; because there's never *"a right time to be in the wrong place."* Trouble can break out anywhere at anytime, but the more information you know about the places you might find yourself, the better decisions you make to avoid potential negative situations.

Things – The things you do to occupy your time is so very important. Idle time invites too much temptation to engage in negativity. People do all kinds of foolishness when bored or have nothing-constructive going on in their life. Find constructive things to occupy your time; school, work, a project, helping others, giving back to your community, involve yourself with a place of worship, workout, spend time with family or read are just a few things you can do can to keep yourself busy.

A Traumatized Life

Most people who have struggled with substance abuse and/or exhibit negative behaviors have suffered some form of trauma in their past. Substance abuse is usually the result of one's attempt to escape the hurt and pain of traumatic experiences. Negative and destructive behavior is usually the result of one's inability to understand and/or process the trauma he or she has experienced. There are two kinds of trauma; the kind that happens to you (physically, emotionally, mentally, verbally and sexually) and the kind that happens around you (violence, crime, death, drugs, gangs, gun violence, domestic violence, and sexual abuse). Trauma experienced at a young age, can leave a lasting emotional scar, well into adult years.

When you're young you don't have the ability to process or understand how trauma is impacting your life and influencing your decisions, but if you take the time to explore and confront the trauma now, you might get to the root of your substance abuse and other negative behavioral issues.

During my incarceration I chose to revisit, explore, and confront the trauma I've experienced in my own life in an effort to understand how trauma may have played a role in my decision-making and negative behavior. People can experience trauma and not even realize it. In most instances, as a survival tactic or trauma coping mechanism, we bury the bad things that have happened to us or around us, in the back of our mind.

For each of traumatic event I have experienced in my life; seeing a friend's mother threaten to jump out a 13 floor window, seeing another friend's mother shot to death by her boyfriend, having two friends die while playing with guns, witnessing fights, stabbings and shootings in my neighborhood regularly, attending several funerals between the ages of 14 and 18, there was never any trauma counseling or trauma centers in my neighborhood to access how these events were impacting me. Where I come from, when things happen you are left to deal with the mental and emotional fallout on your own. Looking back, I see how easy it was for me to become a part of the madness happening around me. By the time I was 21 years old, I was entrenched in a vicious cycle of violence, drug dealing, crime and prison, all of which seemed normal.

Everyone does not and will not deal with trauma in the say way. While it may be hard to recognize if one person has experienced trauma in their life, another person might show signs of aggressiveness, anger, anxiety, difficulty focusing, substance abuse, bitterness, hopelessness, stress, being socially withdrawn, and distrustful of others.

The best way to deal with trauma is to find someone you trust to talk to. Whether it's a trusted friend, family member or trauma counselor, talking about the trauma will release you from the hurt, pain and bad feelings trauma has inflicted on your life, so you can move beyond it.

Your Presentation Game

You've worked on your attitude, managing your anger, overcame bitter, stopped playing the blame game and you're finally taking responsibility for your life. Wow, you've come a long way. You've addressed your shortcomings, faced your fears, strengthened your weaknesses and everyday you're mentally preparing for your release, now it's time to work on your presentation game.

You've worked hard on your internal makeover, now it's time to work just as hard on your external makeover. In most cases we only have one chance to make a first impression so it's important to make that first impression a long lasting one.

Your presentation game consists of appearance, mannerism and how well you articulate yourself. These three things are like the icing on the cake of your change. Your presentation game has the ability to open doors which normally may have been closed to you for various reasons, as well ass keep you locked out of such spaces because of poor presentation.

Your success and livelihood can very well depend on how good your presentation game is. It takes time and practice to sharpen your presentation skills. First you have to visualize how you want the world to see you and then you have to actively work towards being able to project that image. If you can see it, you can be it. Start by upping your vocabulary, reading biographies of successful people and practice speaking without so much street lingo.

Practice your speaking skills on the prison guards and staff until you have your flow down-packed. Then begin practicing your speaking skills on your family and close friends. Don't be afraid how they might react, just tell them the truth; you're trying to learn how to speak so people who don't come from the streets can understand you. You don't have to know or use big words; you just have to be able to communicate clearly.

How you speak around your friends is one thing, how you talk to employer, professionals and people who don't come from or share your experiences is another thing.

I come from the streets and been to prison, but you would never know unless I told you, because I know how to flip my flow to fit the environment I'm navigating through. This is the part where you have to understand you can't take the streets everywhere you go in life. Present yourself, as you want the world to see you, because the way you present yourself is your life's business card.

Ballin' On A Budget

You have to include a budget plan in your new game plan. Budgeting money is something people have trouble with whether they've been incarcerated or not, as a street person you never hear people talking about living on a budget. In the streets you make some money, you spend the money and then you looking for the next scheme, lick or jux to make more money. The money comes fast and it's gone even faster.

How does someone who has never lived on a budget learn how to budget his or her money now? Prison is teaching you how to whether you realize it or not. Most correctional facilities only allow inmates to spend a certain amount of money each month regardless of how much money is in their account, so month-to-month inmates have to budget their money to make sure they have the things they need to survive. Sometimes hours are spent filling out a commissary slip trying to figure out how to get all the things needed from the commissary with a small amount of money, that's how you budget money.

You have to use your money to cover living expenses even when it means sacrificing things that are pleasurable to you. Food, rent, lights, gas, carfare for work, hygiene items and clothes become be your main priorities. Focus on your needs vs. the things you want. Prison teaches you that as well. You might want those brand new sneakers in commissary but those slightly used sneakers being sold in your unit will save you a nice chunk of money you can use to buy your hygiene and food items.

More money more problems. The more your income increases the more the likely you will put less emphasis on sticking to a budget. This is where financial discipline will have to kick in. People often run into financial trouble because of their poor money management skills; not saving for a rainy day. Money management is much more then budgeting for your immediate needs upon release it's about creating a financial plan for your life. Set a financial goal for self; where you want to be financially 5 to 10 years from now and then take the steps you need to get there.

Wasting Valuable Time

We've all heard the saying, *"A mind is a terrible thing to waste"*, but *"time"* is a terrible thing to waste as well.

While you're incarcerated you have nothing but time on your hands why not use that time in a way that benefits you in the future. I consider wasting time doing things that don't contribute to one's positive growth or doesn't contribute to achieving one's goals. You're wasting time if you're not using time to do something that allows you to change your perspective on life.

Trying to come up with the perfect crime or learning how to be a better criminal is a waste of time. Thinking you're going back to society with the same street schemes, street or gangster mentality is a waste of time. Why not use the time you have to do or try something different. Use this time to come up with a different approach because it's apparent, the approach you've had thus far in life is the reason you're incarcerated in the first place. Whether you want to admit it or not, the approach you had to life prior to your incarceration was not the right one.

Take responsibility for your own actions and move on. Wasting time is getting caught up in too many leisurely activities and not spending enough time doing the things that better you. If *ALL* you do is play basketball, if *ALL* you do is watch TV and if *ALL* you do is walk around talking dumb-stuff *ALL* day everyday, then you're definitely wasting your time.

Recreation is supposed to be done in moderation. When you spend more time rec'ing then you do working towards bettering yourself, you need to ask yourself how can I better myself when all I do is rec most of my days away. The same habits you pick up in prison are some of the same habits you'll take to the streets with you. If you can't grasp how precious time is and what you can do with it, then you won't be able to value your time when you go home. Subconsciously going back to prison won't seem so bad of a thing to you.

The only recreational activities I condone 100 percent are playing chess and scrabble. They both enforce certain positive behaviors. Chess puts focus on strategies which you can apply to everyday living and scrabble emphasizes strengthening one's vocabulary. You'll get more life skills playing these games than you'll get playing spades, dominoes, casino or poker on a daily basis.

You won't respect time until you've gone back and forth to prison so much that one day you realize that you've spent most of your life incarcerated. Then you'll regret all the time you've squandered away. You'll look back at your life and have nothing to show for your time on this earth. You'll finally realize how precious time has passed you by. You'll be one of the many brothers who have gone through life merely existing, never knowing what it is to live.

Right now you're at a unique cross-road in your life. You can choose to travel a different road. You can choose to go down the road of change for a better life or you can continue down the road of recklessness and self- destruction. The choice is yours to make. Wasting time is thinking you can do the same things and yield different results. The only way to get different results is to try a different approach. Once you become conscious of the changes you want to make you should wake up every day asking yourself what do I need to do today to change? Once I learned the true value of time, every day I tried to accomplish something no matter how small. You have to discipline yourself on how to spend your time. If you do nothing but go over a thought, review your plan or fine tune an idea, that'll be time well spent.

Wasting time is indulging in frivolous conversation or gossip. The energy spent carrying on these types of conversations could be spent studying. That's time you could be reaching out to someone on the outside and asking them to send you information off the Internet. That wasted energy could be spent doing self-evaluation. The energy spent partaking in frivolous kinds of meaningless talks could be spent reading or expanding on a thought. A non-constructive conversation is a conversation not worth having.

The problem is, dudes do a lot of talking but rarely have positive and constructive things to say. As someone who is learning how to value your time, your antennas should immediately go up when someone approaches you with frivolous conversation. My method for sidestepping dudes like this was to constantly stay busy. If someone tried to stop me for frivolous talk I'd tell them quick I had somewhere to go or had something to do. I always promised to talk to them later. Some people I'd tell straight-up I wasn't trying to hear it or that I wasn't into stuff like that.

Either way dudes will recognize you don't indulge in frivolous talk. Now if it's conversation you can learn from or grow from that's different. When its conversation you can build on or helps you understand something better then you should be all ears. Wasting time is talking about what you use to do or what you used to have on the streets. Talking about the type of person you used to be on the streets. Conversations like that serves no purpose in the larger scheme of life. Instead you should be talking about what you need to do to change before you get back on the streets.

Wasting time is having major drawn-out conversations about rappers, entertainers, athletes or actors and their affairs and financial status. The same people you spend so much time talking about and arguing about won't spend two seconds thinking about brothers caught up in the system. I've seen dudes get into physical confrontations because they disagreed on a rappers ability, financial status or some foolishness like that. This goes back to the sucker who never wants to be wrong.

It's a waste of time knowing everything there is to know about an athlete unless you're going back to society to be a sportscaster. Don't go through your incarceration following the careers or success of others, yet fail to create your own success story. Use another's success story to motivate you. Don't allow yourself to get consumed with what others are doing.

It's a waste of time going through your incarceration professing allegiance to a gang. That nonsense has no room in the future I'm talking to you about. If you have the need to rep something, rep that you were able to break free from the street/prison mentality. How foolish is it for grown men to talk about they're reppin' a neighborhood, city or block? In the larger scheme of life how far can reppin' for your 'hood really get you? When you look back over your life one day, is reppin' for the 'hood or going to prison going to be the best thing you've done with your life?

Playing Catch Up

During your incarceration you will struggle with the past (all the things you did before going to prison), the present (your incarceration) and your future (beyond prison, probation or parole). The past and present will either hold you back or keep you stuck because the future either feels so far away or unreal to you. You will take many trips down memory lane (in your head or during talks with other inmates) because the memories are all you have. It's during those trips back to the past you have to really be careful you don't get stuck wanting to hold on to or relive the past, in the future.

Holding on to the past is one of the thing that causes people to try and play catch up when they are released from prison. Don't spend your time fantasizing about returning to the streets. Leave the past in the past; live in the present preparing for your future.

So many people leave prison trying to play catch up on the streets. They think if they go to enough parties, have enough sex, do enough drugs, catch up with all the latest trends and regain their street status, these things will make up for the time spent in prison. Doing these things is a way to make a person feel like he/she never left, but all it shows is, this person didn't take the time to prepare a plan for getting out.

Playing catch-up is a failed attempt to fill a void that was created while incarcerated because these individuals did not do anything to improve themselves. If you leave prison thinking you can *play catch up* you're setting yourself up for failure.

You can't make up for the time spent behind bars. The best thing to do is make good use of your time while incarcerated, so when you get out you have something positive to show for your time away.

Those who leave prison to play catch up normally don't last long on the streets. If you leave prison respecting the concept of patience your chances of never returning to prison increase immensely. If you didn't have patience before going to prison, you sure know the meaning of patience now; living in an environment where everything is based on controlled movement, that should be enough to teach anyone patience. In prison you have to wait for mail, visits, chow, shower, phone, haircut, an institutional grievance, go to rec, leave rec and so much more. This is the level of patience you have to take home with you.

When you play the catch up game, you allow your wants to be greater than your needs, and once your wants become greater then you have a problem, because all your choices will be based on the things you want and necessarily on the things you need. The things you want should be secondary to the things we need.

Broadening Your Horizon

I spent a lot of time talking to dudes from different countries in order to get an idea of how things were jumpin' off outside of this country. I wanted to learn about the opportunities which existed outside of this country. I also wanted to learn about different cultures and lifestyles. In doing that, it helped me expand my mind. Growing up our culture didn't emphasize or encourage traveling outside the country like other cultures do. As you expand your mind you start having this yearning to see other parts of the world.

I would track down foreign newspapers to read about what's going on in different countries and that kept me abreast of international events. I had visions of doing lots of traveling when I got out. Knowing what was going on in other countries was important. Some dudes only wanna hear news about the 'hood or the streets. We need to learn there's a whole nother world beyond the streets or the 'hood. In order to broaden our horizons we must learn how to get beyond those street and 'hood boundaries.

Give yourself the opportunity to see life beyond the 'hood. Use your time to learn about things going on in the world. You may not think world events affect you but they do. The more you learn and keep abreast about world affairs the better informed and prepared you'll be to face the future.

If you spend your time concerned with 'hood and street events, the probability of you returning to the 'hood or the streets is strong. You have to get past that 'hood and street mentality. You don't wanna return to society wearing your incarceration like a badge of honor. Simply doing a bid isn't something to be proud of. It's what you did *during* your incarceration that brings you pride or shame.

Pride..... Pride that you were able to come home a better person with a strong future. Ashamed... ashamed that you spent all that time away and didn't accomplish jack doo- doo

I stayed abreast of developing technology through reading and tv. I didn't have access to the Internet but I knew enough about it from reading, that when I got home I picked it up instantly. The last institution I was in did offer a beginners course in MS Word which I picked up quickly but other than that I wasn't computer literate at all.

When you come home, one of the first questions people are going to ask you is, what did you do while you were in prison? Your goal should be to leave prison with enough knowledge, direction, and purpose no one can automatically pick up a clue that you were even in prison. Whatever time you're doing, no matter how long, it's your time. The time is your life and how you spend that time reflects how you wanna spend the rest of your life. Don't let time pass you by because you think your current situation is hopeless. The time is what you make it and what you take from it.

One day the prison doors will open and one day you'll go home. You don't wanna face that day unprepared. Many people have faced their release date not knowing what they were gonna do when they get out. Make it your goal to be someone who faces their release day with plans and confidence of what the future has to offer. Go back to society a better person, a changed person, a very determined person. Don't waste your time. Have something to show for all the years you have been incarcerated.

Building Your Character

Don't let anyone tell you that prison doesn't or can't build character in a man. You know better! Prison is one of the few places left where a man's word still means something or better mean something. Without your word in the prison environment you'll have problems eventually. When you give your word in prison you better be able to back your word up because if you're unable to, it could lead to serious trouble. When you tell someone you're going to do something you do it; from repaying a debt to meeting up later with them. In prison we go on someone's word because it's the only thing we have that we're still in control of.

Liars get no respect in prison. Dudes take lying real serious. Lying is something that can get you in trouble. You always have the dudes who lie about what they had on the streets; all the money, cars and women. Dudes don't even realize how much more respected they'd be if they weren't pretending to be someone they were not. Be yourself, whatever you were, whatever you did and whatever you had is not important. What is important is, who are you today. What are you doing today to prepare for the future?

In prison your survival can depend on your character and if your character doesn't garner any respect, then you very well can find yourself in trouble. Prison teaches you how to respect others, their property, their beliefs, and most of all their space. Prison teaches you, if you respect others – others will respect you (most times). The prison culture is run on respect one way or another.

The same way your survival in prison can depend on your character, your success in society can also depend on your character. People out here wanna know they can trust you. That when you say something you mean it. They wanna feel confident you'll do what you say. The same character traits which get you through prison are the same character traits that can help you as you try to accomplish your goals out here.

People in the legitimate world shun the same negative character traits that are shunned in the prison environment. Though the results are different, you still can get hurt when your character isn't right out here, you hurt your chances. When people don't wanna deal with you because of your character, you lose and your chances of succeeding diminish. Trust me, when people see you're a straight up person just out to do the right thing, doors will open for you.

Having the ability to articulate yourself, your thoughts and your point of view without using street language should be a very big part of your character. No matter how wrong it is, people often judge or perceive you based upon the way you articulate yourself. When you're out here trying to meet and network with people you have to be conscious of how you speak. Being able to speak articulately might be the determining factor whether someone chooses to hire you, do business with you or opens a much needed door for you. From the time you open your mouth, what you say and how you say it might determine how far you're able to go out here. For some of us, learning how to speak without all the street and/or jail vernacular is like learning how to talk again. It's cool because practice makes perfect. Stay conscious of how you speak and don't be afraid to check yourself. You'll slowly but surely develop a knack to flip between speaking street and mainstream English.

When you're out here on your legal grind there's a certain code of ethics you must learn to abide by. One of the main things that help you to succeed out here is your character. Tear up that *code of the streets* guide you've been going by, in the real world it's a whole different ball game and you play by different rules.

Your character should speak louder than words can speak about you. People look at your character to see who you really are and what you're really about. People already look at us skeptically because of our past but when you show you've built character over the years the old image of you fades and the new person you are becomes the dominant image.

Accepted Ignorance

As you grow during your journey of change, you'll begin to see a lot of things for what they really are. Especially when it comes to your thinking. A lot of us never even realized how we fell victim to accepted ignorance and once we fell victim to it we promoted it.

Accepted ignorance is the mentality that leads us to believe that living the street life is cool. That doing whatever illegal act you have to do to make a fast dollar is cool *because the end justifies the means* (which is a load of crap), even if the end means prison or death. Accepted ignorance is believing you can hustle your way outta the 'hood. It's that mentality which makes us idolize and respect pimps, drug dealers and Italian mobsters. It's that mentality which makes us invest more money into looking good then we invest into living good.

It was these twisted ways of thinking that blinded a lot of us. I remember when I was young I had a uncle named Junior/June bug. I thought he was the hippest and coolest dude alive. He'd tell me things like *"the working man is a sucker" "you have to have a hustle out here" "if it don't make dollars it don't make sense" "pimps up birds down"*. He'd always have a pocket full of money and to me he was the man. Little do I know, dudes like him and countless other images of male ghetto glory were planting the seeds for me to think I could conquer the streets too. At the time I thought I was being schooled to the *game*, but the only thing I was being schooled on was, how to fail.

We got our criminal cues from images we seen in movies like Super Fly, The Mack and later on Scarface, King of New York and Good Fellas. We followed the careers of big time drug dealers like Nicky Barnes and Guy Fisher. We were mesmerized by infamous mobsters like Lucky Luciano, Al Capone and later on John Gotti.

We allowed ourselves to believe that going to prison was part of the so-called *game*. The price you paid for doing business. Accepted ignorance is saying, *"the streets is all I know"* or *"the only thing I know how to do is hustle."* These are only excuses used to justify your continuous negative and illegal behavior. These sayings only state your unwillingness to try or learn something different.

The same criminal entities we idolized and respected so dearly, are some of the same criminal entities who had been pumping our communities with destruction and death for the longest. We blindly became their aiders and abettors in the destruction of our own when we adopted their criminal codes of honor, their criminal ethics and their criminal greed.

Rappers further exacerbated the situation by encouraging young people to live their lives according to the streets. Rappers adopted, exploited and sold young people the same street life images they were getting from dudes like us. There's a saying that goes, *"a real rapper doesn't hustle and a real hustler doesn't rap."* For the sake of making money a lot of rappers tried harder and harder to come across as being a real street dude. In doing so, rappers sold a whole generation of young people an illusion of the street life. While dudes like us were getting a hun'ned years in prison or getting killed, rappers were talking about what they were doing from the safety of a studio. With the constant bombardment of negativity, a whole generation has been indoctrinated in the ways of accepted ignorance. People are dying and going to prison under the guise of *'keepin' it street, gangsta, real, and 'hood."*

First came the heroin, then the crack and now it's the rap. Rap has had far worse effects on our community then heroin and crack combined. With hip hop's images of street life; *drug dealing, drug usage, criminal behaviors, gang activity, reckless sex, and violence* a whole generation has bought into this ill fated illusion of what it means to be street, cool, a baller, and a thug. Rappers rap about a lifestyle they don't live and make millions. We live a lifestyle rappers rap about and receive a million years.

One of the most profound things that happens on your journey to change is you begin to think and see a lot of things differently. Your mind begins to reject accepted ignorance and starts to reject the street life, street mentality, and prison mentality. These things now become unaccepted ignorance.

It's time for brothers like us to "STAND UP!" and say, *enough is enough.* Rappers wouldn't have anything to rap about if we all decided to change our game plan.

This Jail Is Sweet

can't tell you how many times I've heard guys make that statement while I was incarcerated. Dudes would tell

people on the outside how supposedly sweet the prison they were in was all the time. No matter how many televisions, microwaves, state-of-art amenities you find in prison, no prison is sweet. How can prison be sweet when you don't have your freedom? Brothers are being conditioned to accept their confinement because they have a few creature comforts. No jail or prison is sweet and when you allow yourself to think jail or prison is sweet then you're preconditioning yourself to coming back. When you think of any place as being sweet, don't you wanna go back to that place? Don't you miss that place when you're not there? When the pressures of the free world begin to overwhelm you and trust me they will, you'll begin to reminisce on how "sweet" jail was and how "sweet" you had it in prison. Get that 'this prison is sweet' mentality out your head.

When you tell people, especially young people, on the outside how sweet a prison is or how sweet you have it in prison, you're sending the wrong message. Bad enough young people already have the wrong perception of what prison is all about, we don't need brothers telling them prison is sweet. All that does is precondition them to see prison as being something cool. You have to be aware of the messages that you send out to the streets when you're locked down. Young people are very impressionable and easily influenced.

The part of society that wants to keep you locked up and mentally enslaved does all it can do to make you feel that prison is sweet. They'll invest in a lot of frivolous creature comforts to keep you blind to your own suffering. They've gotten so good at it that some new prisons are being built

Changin' Your Game Plan 111

to resemble college campuses. I've been to a couple maximum security prisons where you'd swear you were at some type of cottage village. I swear to you. They've designed prisons now that you don't even see the actual walls or fences. The newer prisons are much cleaner and come with a lot of state-of-the-art technology.

Always be mindful of where you are. Never allow yourself to think or feel any prison is sweet. Freedom is sweet. Doing something positive with your life is sweet. Being out here with your family and loved ones is sweet.

Baby Mama/Wifey Drama

It's hard enough doing time, but when you have to go through changes with the mother of your child, it makes doing time much harder. Unfortunately that's also part of doing time. A lot of brothers don't wanna admit that they weren't good to their kid's mother when they were out there, so when she decides to go left on'em he wants to get mad. It's a bitter pill to swallow but it's the truth. You might have been looking out for your baby mother (and a lot of brothers weren't even doing that), but you still wasn't treating her fair. Most of us had other women on the side. We thought calling our baby mother our main girl was good enough for her. Now we flip out when the shoe's on the other foot. We're wrong for giving our baby mothers grief from prison when we weren't right by them on the streets. It's not fair. Those days of having our cake and eating it too are over.

Just because a woman has a child by you doesn't mean she has to accept being treated foul by you. At first it'll be hard for you to accept this, foolish pride kicking in, but as you grow you'll take responsibility for your actions. If you were out there messing around on your baby's mom then you should be mad at yourself, not her. Women don't wanna hear that their man or their kid's father loves them when he goes to jail, they wanna feel loved when their man is on the streets. By the time your street life catches up to you, you've already burned so many bridges with your girl, prison becomes that escape hatch she's been praying for. When brothers get locked up they wanna forget all the drama they took their woman through before going away. Prison doesn't outweigh your mistreatment of your baby's mom.

Dudes walk around prison all gangster'd out, but as soon as they call home and found out wifey isn't home or wifey kickin' it with the next dude they ready to hurt someone or worse hurt themselves. You can't go to prison and suddenly cry (literally) for your lady if you weren't treating your lady right.

Remember this, the true strength of a man is in his ability to stand on his own two feet. Women ridicule brothers who go to prison and cry that lovey dovey talk when he wasn't talking it on the streets.

I was talking about that earlier, guys don't wanna take responsibility for their actions so they blame the woman. It might be hard to accept but it's the truth. The best thing you can do is try to maintain a friendship with your baby's mom for the sake of the kids. Don't get in her business like she didn't get in yours while you were on the streets.

When it comes to all the other women, you gotta let them know off top, *"with or without you I gotta do this time. You can holla when you holla, but I'm not gonna sweat you while I'm away."* Let them rollout if that's what they wanna do. In order for you to get through this situation with a clear head and a positive outlook you have to drop dead weight. Anybody who's bringing drama to your life is dead weight. Stressin' over them chicks while you're lock- down is what messes a lot of brothers head up.

Now is the time to be a bigger man than you were before you went away. Instead of trying to get in your baby's mother's business, let her know whatever transpires between you two while you're away, you'll always be there for her. Even if it's nothing more then being someone she can talk to. Let her go on with her life. Let her find out what's really good out there and if she makes her way back to you, then try and build a real relationship with her. Give baby's mom and/or wifey the time and space she needs as well as deserves. Let the chips fall where they may. You never wanna put pressure on a woman to stick with you. If your baby's mom or any woman decides to stick by you, let it be a decision she makes from her heart and not because she feels you're a charity case.

I don't make excuses for myself or any man. You have a choice, make excuses or make change, but you can't do both. I'm giving it to you real. I'm not with that self-pity crap. Everything that happens is a direct result of the lifestyles we chose to live. I wasn't crying when I felt like I was on top of the world so I wasn't about to cry when I hit rock bottom. I had too much pride for that. All I kept thinking was how was I going to come back from all of this.

Dudes like to get mad when I give it to them real like this. When guys start talking about how their baby's mom, girl or wifey was treating them I wouldn't give them a shoulder to cry on. Instead I'd ask the hard questions that bring the truth out. I'm not gonna let you beat me in head like you're the victim, when there's a strong chance you were treatin' women foul. Guys only wanna tell you what they want you to know. A lot of dudes were treating women real foul out there. Admitting you weren't playing fair with women is the first step to accepting responsibility for your actions.

Women get tired too you know. A woman wants a man who's gonna be there for her and be there with her. After they've been through enough nonsense with the thugs and street dudes they start looking for that square dude who we took to be the sucker. Woman are looking for dudes like this to settle down with. That's the way life goes. After it's all said and done, the only thing the street dude is left with is a gang of time or with some dirt in his mouth (death).

Dudes who run the streets don't have a future and women know that. Fall-back and let your baby's mom or your girl/ wifey do her thing while you take the time to get yourself straight. If y'all were meant to be together then time can't change that. You wanna have yourself together in the event y'all wanna see if y'all could have something going on again. Regardless of what happens, remember, you left her out there.

There is also something very important to figure in during your positive journey. After a man starts walking down that road of change in a lot of cases he doesn't even want the same type of women he was dealing with before he got locked up.

Remember, when you change you're not only seeing life differently. You start to see people differently as well. I guarantee you, your perception of the kind of women you want to deal with will definitely change.

Knowing A Good Woman's worth

One of brothers main distractions when they're released from prison is women. Most guys get out of prison and the first thing they start looking for is sex. Making sex your first priority upon release will be your biggest mistake. When you get out of prison the first thing you should concentrate on is, putting your life back together. Making sure you're doing the things that will put you on stable ground. Running around trying to sex a bunch of women for the sake of having sex is counterproductive to achieving your goals.

The time will come when you'll be in a position to meet and become intimate with women. Again, you want to be in a strong position when that time comes. When you start interacting with women you want them to know you have something to bring to the table other than wanting sex. You also want a good woman to know you have something else on your mind other than sex.

When dating women becomes a part of your life, you wanna be able to interact with the type of women who are about something. This way, if you become emotionally involved with a good woman, the two of you can build something solid together. You have to be able to give a good woman a look at the vision that you have created.

To come home and have sex for the sake of having sex is a waste of time, not to mention dangerous. You meet a woman, you're fresh out of prison, you don't know anything about this woman's background, sexual history, or if she has the HIV virus. Exercising patience will eventually lead you to the kind of woman that you really can build something with instead of having fly-by-night relationships which mean absolutely nothing.

The only chance brothers like us have of getting with a good woman when we get out is, if we have our life together. While we're off somewhere doing time in prison, a lot of the same women we used take for granted are out there stepping their games up getting married, raising kids, pursuing careers and acquiring wealth. The only chance guys like us have now of getting with some of these same women who used to be infatuated with us, is having something more substantial going on other then the lifestyle we used to live.

It has to be a crushing experience for a man to run into a woman he used to deal with back in the days and now she's embarrassed to acknowledge having dealt with him. Street dudes don't get any play with these women anymore. Women are older now, they want stability now, so all that other superficial stuff doesn't get it with them anymore.

A good woman will give a brother like us the benefit of doubt but he has to be able to give a woman some sort of blueprint of what he's trying to do with his life. There's a lot of good women out here but they've been through the street guy phases of their life and now they're looking for a whole lot more.

These days when a brother goes away most times he won't be coming home until he's in his mid thirties or forties. Women at this age aren't into the same games and nonsense they used to be into back in the days. They don't accept the games dudes used to run on them back in the days.

I went to a nice little after work spot with one of my old friends. A honey from his job had a little birthday gathering at this spot in mid-town and there were women all over the place. I mean nice grown and sexy women. It was a nice mature crowd, laid back and the women were looking good. I had the pleasure to meet a couple women, one was a lawyer, a banker and the secretary of the Queens Borough president.

I met a couple of college administrators and a high school guidance counselor. All the while I'm conversing with these together sisters not one of them had any idea I had just came home from doing thirteen and a half years. When I'm telling these women what I do for a living the reception was positive and encouraging.

My brothers when you get out here, you wanna be able to interact with women who have things going on. When it comes to achieving your goals it's always good and necessary to network with people and especially women because they hold some of the influential positions in corporate America. The way I used to be with the women back in the days.... I wasn't about to come out here and let any woman look down on me. I can only imagine how it will be for some brothers when they're the brunt of the *"I wonder what happened to so-and-so"* jokes when old girlfriends get together. Or the *"I seen so-and-so downtown the other day and girl he looks lost/bad/ through"*. And you know how women can and will rip a guy apart when rubbing his failures in.

This Ain't A Game

I want you to get your head right while you're away. With brothers like us out here building on the moves I'm putting into motion it won't be long before we carve out our piece of the pie legitimately this time. It's not too late for us. I'm trying to set up things so when it's time for brothers to get out they can step right into something positive.

You might get tired of me preaching but I plan to beat you over head with these jewels until I know you're taking everything I'm saying serious. This ain't no game. Things are serious out here. If you don't get right, the system will lock your butt up and throw away the key. We're already at a disadvantage coming home with a felony. It's not like back in the days when you could do two-three bids and still come home semi-young. Now when you catch a felony, a second or third felony you're lucky if you make home before you turn fifty, let-alone make it home at all. I know dudes still doing time from the late eighties early nineties who won't be coming home until 2015, 2020, 2025 not even talking about the ones doing life. All this time because of drugs.

Having been to prison carries a negative stigma in society but it's not something that can't be overcome. Have the determination to show society that you have what it takes to come out on top in the worst of situations. If you can turn things around for yourself you will have accomplished something only a few people are able to do. You will be counted among some of the great people who have overcome all kinds of adversity. Once you have bettered yourself and you're doing things that are positive and you've become successful, people aren't going to dwell on the fact that you've been to prison. It's going to be about what you're doing now. Your present actions are what you'll judged by.

All these things should be a factor when you decide you've had enough and its time to change your life around. You're supposed to look at all the dudes who won't ever have a chance to walk the streets again and be thankful everyday that you have a second chance. A second chance at freedom after everything you've done. To come home and take freedom for granted by jumping back out in the streets is a waste. Because when the day comes, and it will come, that the judge finally gets tired of seeing your face in his courtroom, you're going to wish to God you would've changed your game plan when you had the opportunity to. I've been around brothers who wish they had a chance to go home and do anything, work in McDonalds, be a messenger, wash cars, it wouldn't matter.

A lot of these brothers are some good brothers too. They're just messed up in the system right now. Some of the hardest guys there is in the prison system have told me they wish they had just one more chance to do the right thing in society. I thank God everyday, every time I wake up, for giving me an opportunity to get back out here and make something of myself. I'm not about to throw away my second chance at life. When dudes tried to clown me about getting soft I wasn't trippin'. When dudes found out I was writing and making plans for the future, a lot of them started hatin' on me. I wasn't worryin' about it though, you know why? Because I stopped caring what anybody had to say about me. When it comes down to it, I have to live with me not with what someone thinks about me.

Dudes used to call me square, lame, a nerd and I used to laugh to myself because these was the same dudes who just didn't get it. These were the same dudes who'd be running around the jail like they were still on the streets. Every time a new pair of sneakers came out in the commissary they had to have them. Every new item, from radio to sweat suits they had to have it. These were the same dudes who were trying to get women to smuggle weed into the jail for them.

These were the dudes who still felt they had something to prove and still felt their worth was based on materialistic value. These were the same dudes who called themselves judging me......??? Please! Ask how many of these dudes sent money home to their kid and they'd all tell you *'my kid is being well taken care of'.* That wasn't the point brother, you're up in here trying to play fly guy, Mr. Mackdocious yet you won't send your kid a couple dollars just to let him/her know their father was thinking about them. Was I gonna let these type of dudes discourage me from reaching new heights? No Sir! I knew a dude who wouldn't even write his kids let alone send them anything. He said he didn't write them because they didn't write him. Wow! Yet this same dude was running around the jail like he was on Big Willie status. A lot of dudes' priorities are just plain messed up when it comes to prison. Even if your kids never respond to your letters write them because it will become an issue later on if you don't write.

I'd get mad when I would hear some of the plans dudes had when they get out. Believe it or not, a lot of dudes find no shame in saying they're going back out to the world to hustle illegally. I used to be buggin'. Here's a dude who is in prison for drugs, had his freedom taken away for drugs, and still he can't wait to get out so he can sell drugs again. I found that mentality incredible. You always hear dudes use the excuses, *'when I get out there my kids gotta eat'*. And you know what I used to say to that? *"Ain't your kids eaten' now? You not out there. I don't see nobody writing you saying that your kids are hungry, so miss me with the lies. You going out to get money for you, not your kids."* Sad to say, but a lot of brothers are using their kids as excuses to get back out there in the street life. Some dudes would tell you straight up they're going back out in the streets to get money. I used to tell them dudes, *"you got more balls than me cause I can't do this prison thing again."*

Just hearing how other brothers have been trapped off and the amount of time they were getting hit with was enough for me to call the streets quits. It's not worth it anymore, not that it was ever worth it. What you have to ask yourself is, is anything about the street lifestyle worth the time you wind up spending away? The time you have to spend away from your family and away from your kids? At the end of the day it's just not worth it. Take the dude who's in prison for selling drugs and he's in prison selling drugs. How mind boggling is that? What will it take for him to get it, three or four trips to prison? How does a guy explain to his family and to his kids that he caught another case and prison sentence while *'in'* prison? Don't let yourself get sucked into the false reality of prison life.

Drafting A New Game Plan

What happens when you're on the street trying to get money illegally and nothing you try seems to work? No matter what you do or try you're constantly coming up empty handed. You go back to your criminal drawing board and try to come up with the next street scheme or street hustle. You say to yourself, *"yo, I need to change my game plan! This ain't workin' out."* Simply put, you start over. This is the same concept, only this time you're changin' your game plan to do something positive and productive on the street, things that'll keep you out of prison.

When you start drafting your new game plan make a list of all the things you're good at. From your ability to fast talk people to your knack for remembering things. If you have a thing for detail, being punctual or getting the job done put it on your list. Are you a problem solver, a people person or a good negotiator? Can you improvise, are you a team player or can you perform under pressure? List any unique skills or talents that you possess. Once you've made your list you have to find a way to incorporate the things on your list in to your new game plan. Some of these things you'll use immediately and some things you'll use as needed.

In order to not only make it but to be successful out here you have to know how to sell yourself and emphasize the things about you that set you apart from everyone else. Focus on those things that make you unique and use those things to your advantage. You have to make everything on your list work for you. You may possess a unique experience which you can also draft a new game plan around. Everyone has something unique about themselves. You may have a canny knack to come up with unique ideas or invent unique things. Whatever it is, you have to find a way to capitalize on all the things you know, been through, or are good at.

What makes me an expert on prison? The thirteen years, six months and two days that I spent incarcerated. What makes me an expert on change? The journey I embarked on to change. All I did was use something I knew a lot about from firsthand experience and used that firsthand experience to write this book.

Everyone has some type of special skill, niche or unique angle. It's about being able to find a market where you can turn your special skill, niche or unique angle into revenue. Talking that slick street talk allowed me to write my first book: **STREET TALK: *Da Official Guide to Hip-Hop & Urban Slanguage.*** Making major changes while incarcerated and preparing myself for the future while incarcerated allowed me to write, **Changin' Your Game Plan.**

Take a person who knows the stickup game, he can turn that around and become a security consultant who goes around showing people and establishments how to be better secure. He can give pointers on spotting suspicious behavior, explaining how criminals think, and what would be the best and most cost effective way to secure one's person or property. Now you get a chance to exploit your criminal skills. The same criminal acts that used to get you in trouble can now be used as an asset. What makes you an expert? You're hands on experience in committing robbery. If someone's criminal forte is burglary they'd have intimate knowledge of breaking into someone's home or business, so who better to advise people on taking protective measures.

You still have to do your homework. Do research on the latest high tech security measures from the inexpensive to the high end stuff so you'll be able to recommend security solutions within a wide range of budgets. And that's only one example how you can incorporate something you know a lot about into your new game plan. Remember, drafting a new game plan is more then planning what you're gonna do when you get out, it's also about what you're doing while you're *in* to prepare for getting out.

When you're incarcerated you're at a unique juncture in your life. Very seldom do people get the opportunity to draft a new game plan for their life in mid-stream. People either become content or locked into a certain situation that prevents them from pursuing their lifelong passions. Most people go to work every day and hate their job. Most people wish they were doing something else. A lot of people just give into whatever they're doing to earn a living and let go of their dreams.

People's immediate responsibilities don't allow them to stop what they're doing to draft another game plan. They hold on to what brings in income and stick with that because of the security it brings them.

For the person coming out of incarceration, he's free to do whatever he sets his heart out to do. After his release he doesn't have the same immediate responsibilities the average person on the street has. A guy coming home doesn't have the same pressures as a dude who has been on the streets raising his family. When you first come home most people will understand you have to get yourself together before you can contribute to anyone else's well-being. During that window you'll have at the least a couple months to get your plans off the ground.

Where some guys go wrong is, thinking since they've been away, they deserve to do nothing for a while. The faster you get on your grind the faster you can implement your game plan.

At the same time you're drafting your new game plan, you're also creating a vision. The vision you set for yourself is the blueprint of what you're striving to achieve. When I started down the road of change I began to envision myself doing a lot of different things I never even imagined of doing before. The more I learned about different things and different way of doing things I started telling myself, *you can do that*. I began to have different visions and ideas of what I was going to do when I left prison.

Sometimes the visions you have, people on the outside won't be able to see, comprehend or believe. From experience, you have to be careful who you share your thoughts and visions with. When it comes down to it, as long as you believe in your visions that's all that matters. Staying focused and passionate about those visions will also help keep you motivated during your incarceration.

Creating the vision in your mind is the first step, working toward making that vision a reality is the second step and implementing that vision when you get home is the final step. You have to strive toward that vision every day. I would eat and sleep my visions. Everything I did in some way contributed to the cultivation of my visions.

Constructive Criticism

How many of us can accept criticism? Not many. We all like to criticize others, but when it comes to being criticized we don't like it. Who wants to hear somebody telling them what's wrong with them? As far as we're concerned we're good. It's our stubborn refusal to accept criticism that keeps us from looking at criticism as another tool we could use to better ourselves. You might not want to hear and accept when someone offers criticisms about you, but you know when what's being said is true. Especially when more then one person has the same criticisms about you.

Constructive criticism is criticism by someone who cares about you and wants you to be your best. It's a plus when you can take constructive criticism and apply it positively to your life. A part of growing is about being open to constructive criticism.

After I finished my first book STREET TALK I sent it to a lot of literary agents and I happened to catch the attention of one. He was very excited about what I'd done and believed the book had strong potential. He was very enthusiastic about wanting to help me get a publishing deal. He sent the manuscript to a publishing editor over at Doubleday and we were both excited about the possibility of me getting a book deal so soon with a major publishing house.

Well needless to say the editor from Doubleday sent the manuscript back to the literary agent with a rejection letter. Of course I was very disappointed, but when I received a copy of the rejection letter I was more angry then anything. The editor had pointed out so many things that were wrong with the book it crushed my spirit something terrible. I fumed over the rejection letter for a week or two, when after speaking to the literary agent one day about the rejection he gave me some very valuable jewels. He said, "stop looking at the letter as rejection but a tool to make the book better. Use all the points from the letter and see how you could incorporate them into the book to make it better. Go back to the drawing board and send me a book I can sell."

I was guilty of doing what a lot of people do when they're criticized, they take it personal. I had falsely felt the publishing editor was rejecting my work because she felt it had no merit but all the while she was rejecting it because it needed to be more organized, reader friendly and more in-depth. Once I was able to accept the constructive criticism it allowed me to revise STREET TALK. If you compared the original manuscript to the manuscript it is today you'll agree the original one needed major work done on it. Today I'm grateful for the rejection of the original manuscript because it forced me to understand and grasp the concept of constructive criticism.

Of course all criticism isn't constructive, but if given from a friend or loved one who has no hidden agenda or ulterior motives then you should be open to looking at what's being said about you. A friend or loved one is going to point out your weaknesses and then tell what you need to do to strengthen them. When they criticize you they won't do it with malice or as away to hurt and down you.

Friends help each other be the best they can be.

Facing Your Fears

Too many brothers allow fear to stop them from applying self-analysis techniques. Fear of having to face themself and the demons they may have created. The fear of not knowing whether they can make the changes to be a better person. There is also the fear of leaving a part of oneself behind to make way for the new person making their way to the forefront. Fear cripples a lot of brothers in prison. Dudes would rather be one of the status quo walking around doing nothing constructive because they're too afraid to be different. You can't let fear stop you from moving forward. Put that fear behind you. Fear is a struggle that you have to overcome. Overcoming fear helps to build self-confidence. A lot of times we allow fear to become more then it is, then the fear grows into its own monster.

You know what I feared more than anything else? Returning to prison. I heard a lot of dudes say, *"I got another bid in me."* But what I used to wonder is, does your mom have another bid in her, what about your kids or people who care about you? I knew I didn't have another bid in me so change was the only option.

Whether we like it or not, sometimes change is forced upon us. It's at that point we have to decide whether or not to accept the challenge to change. If a doctor said, *"smoke another cigarette and you will die"*, would you have that last cigarette? Some people would, even knowing the consequences. Me, I'd have to quit. Same thing with prison, the judge basically told me, if he sees me in his courtroom again that I'd never see the streets again. If I didn't get it after receiving fifteen years in, then the system was saying, I didn't deserve anymore chances to get it. Each bid gets worse and worse until you box yourself in and wind up faced with the rest of life in prison because you kept coming back.

Prisons aren't being built to temporarily house brothers anymore, they're being built to permanently house brothers. They're locking brothers up young and not letting them out until they're in their late fifties and sixties. Change was the only option for me.

Change is good and nothing to be feared. Anything you do for the first time is going to be a little scary. For some brothers who are trying to better themselves, change is something new to them. Some brothers have done and thought about doing wrong for so long it seems like the natural thing to do. To break away from that mind-frame has to be a little scary. But like any new experience, once you figure out there's nothing to be scared of, you learn to be better at the same thing you once feared.

Facing and overcoming fear helps to improve yourself. It gives you a chance to look at yourself in different way. The way I conquered my fear of coming back to prison was easy, I decided not to put myself in situations that could or would lead me to going back to prison. I decided I was done with committing crimes of any nature.

Believing In Yourself

When you find yourself going through trials and tribulations it's hard to believe you can turn circumstances around and do something positive. You do wrong for so long it's like that's all you know how to do. If no one believes in you, you have to believe in yourself and believe in the changes you're making for yourself. How much you believe in yourself will determine whether you succeed or fail out here. Believing in yourself is about having confidence in yourself. Believe just because you've made some mistakes doesn't mean you can't do better.

When I had reached the lowest point in my life I didn't know what the future had in store for me. As I began down the road of change I started believing that I could turn things around for myself. You can have and make all the plans in the world, but if you don't believe in yourself, everything you do is done without the full confidence you'll need to succeed. Plans and goals are only accomplished when one believes he/she can accomplish them.

You'll come across lots of people who'll try to discourage you and knock you for the changes you're striving to make. You have to stand strong when faced with doubters. Let belief in yourself be the shield that protects you from doubtfulness. Brother, when you truly believe in yourself it's an exhilarating feeling. I never doubt myself or the things I'm doing because I approach everything believing that, as long as I put the hard work into what I'm doing I'll accomplish my objective.

Keep telling yourself every chance you get, *"I can do this, I can do this."* I read somewhere that a man is literally what he thinks. If you think negative thoughts you'll be negative. If you think positive thoughts you'll see yourself as being a positive person. It's always nice to have people who believe in you. Ultimately it comes down to what you believe about yourself.

Preparing to Fail

For all the brothers going through their incarceration preparing to go to the streets to use their prison experience as a means to intimidate, bully, or muscle their way around be warned. Many brothers have left with these same negative ambitions and have wound up another statistic. The statistic that keeps track of those who have left prison only to go home and be killed.

There are a lot of brothers walking around prison right now with the misconception that the world, the 'hood, or society owes them something. These dudes have the attitude that if what they think is owed to them isn't given willingly they're going to take it. This mind-frame has sent a lot of newly released prisoners to their grave. If you think the streets owe you something because you did time you're preparing to fail. If you think you know what it takes *"this time"* to be a successful criminal then you're preparing to fail.

If you think you're going home to reclaim your block, your 'hood or some criminal scheme before you went to prison you're preparing to fail. When you leave prison with the attitude the streets owe you something often the payment is death.

Nine times out of ten if you look at those dudes who have left prison only to go home and be killed and you look at the way they did their time, the great majority of them didn't do anything constructive with their time. As soon as they were released they went right back to the behaviors they knew best;

hanging out with the same people, in the same areas, doing the same things.

Thinking people will automatically fear you because you've been to the penitentiary is how a lot of brothers wound up dead when they left prison. While you've been away new dudes have moved in to fill the shoes of those who are sent to prison. Right now the street are preparing for dudes like you who think they're gonna come home and take over something or muscle people around. Others have staked a claim to the same streets you ran once upon a time and just like you back then, they're not about to give up an inch because you just come home from prison. If you're spending time trying to build your criminal ties you're preparing to fail. If you and the dudes you hang with in prison are consciously making plans to meet up on the outside to further criminal acts then you're preparing to fail.

The things you find yourself doing while incarcerated are a lot of the same things you'll find yourself doing when you're released back to society. If you don't take the time to change while incarcerated then you're preparing to fail. If you're involved in gang activity while in prison you're preparing to fail. Gang life won't get you far when you get out of prison. Run with gangs and eventually you'll find yourself indulging in criminal activity again where you'll either return to prison or wind up dead.

If you fail to break away from negativity while you're incarcerated you're preparing to fail. If you think the reputation you had on the streets or while you were in prison is going to take you far when you get out then you're preparing to fail.

138

If you're depending on someone to give you something when you're released then you're preparing to fail. Prepare to make your own way upon release and use whatever someone gives you as an added bonus. If you do nothing for yourself while locked up because someone promised to take care of you when you get out you're preparing to fail. You know the saying, *'momma may have - pappa may have - but god blesses the child who has his own'*. Make sure you do the things to secure your own future first before depending on what someone says they'll do for you.

Brothers have to stop going home with an expectation that people are going to hand them something when they get out. They failed to prepare for their future. They're left with no plan now that they're back in society. You can't be left out in the cold if you've taken time to prepare yourself for your eventual return to society. Preparing yourself to win means learning how to humble yourself. Not walking around with a chip on your shoulder. Not being able to be humble often causes a lot of different problems for brothers when they come home. Being humble means not feeling you have to be confrontational or unwilling to back down because you don't want to be seen as soft or a sucker. Not learning the art of humbleness is another way how dudes prepare to fail.

While guys around you do nothing to better themselves, strive to change and prepare yourself for the future. If you go through your incarceration with thoughts of hustling again then you're preparing to fail. Do yourself some justice and make positive changes in your life. Learn what it really means to live a fulfilling and rewarding life. Those who fail to prepare *for* the future, only prepare to fail *in* the future.

Using prison as an Asset

Believe it or not, your prison experience can be an asset in society if you know how to present it properly. Your plan is only as good as the way you market and present it. People are extremely receptive to a brother who has been through the system and has taken the journey of change. People love to hear stories of brothers who have overcome the prison obstacle, endured the struggle and come home a better man. You'd be surprised how many doors will open for you and how many people will offer their support when they're confident that your change is genuine. People like to get behind a underdog because so many people can relate to struggle.

When people see the change in one of us, it offers them hope that their friend, family member or love one will or can change as well. I don't wear my prison experience as a badge of honor, nor do I run from it. Part of who I am today is a direct result of me spending so much time incarcerated. You can't imagine how many people have responded positively to me when I approach them with a flyer for this book. It's a very satisfying feeling to have strangers encourage you. People aren't concerned with what you've done in the past. What concerns them most is, what are you doing now. There's not a person alive who doesn't have something in their past that they wish they could change or undo. Making mistakes is what makes us human.

Your prison experience only becomes an asset when you're doing something positive with yourself. Take someone who does the same thirteen and a half years like me, yet comes home without a plan and exhibits the same negative behaviors he had before going away. As soon as people see this guy hasn't changed, they'll keep their distance. It might sound corny but it's true and I can bear witness to this. You get much more respect when you're doing something positive then you get when you're doing something negative. In life, if you don't know the value of an asset you wind up losing it.

Misery Loves Company

As we all know, there's a lot of miserable brothers in prison. I mean MIS-ER-ABLE! Guys like this you have to stay far away from. Their misery has a way of infecting everyone around them. I know prison isn't the best place to be in the world, but true leaders will rise above their circumstances and make the best of any situation. Even situations they put themselves in. To wake up miserable every day, walk around miserable all day, and to make it your mission to make dudes around you miserable uses way more energy than it takes to better yourself.

Most dudes are miserable because they don't know what else to be but miserable. They haven't looked for or discovered an outlet for all that built up anger and bitterness that keeps them so miserable. Brothers hold on to those negative emotions because they feel it's the right or expected way to feel under the circumstances. If everyone around you is miserable chances are, you'll learn to be miserable too. The brothers who aren't walking around in a state of constant misery become something of an anomaly. Someone others can't figure out.

When you decide to make those much needed changes in your life you'll discover you don't have time to be miserable because you're too busy preparing for the future. You'll see a brighter and better future for yourself. You'll discover being miserable is wasted energy. Energy you can use to move ahead positively. You'll also discover living in a constant state of misery is like succumbing to the notion that you can't do better so why try.

Misery is another way to admit defeat; it's the equivalent of giving up on oneself. Misery keeps you from seeing anything positive or constructive in your future. Misery is to let external factors dictate whether or not you take the necessary steps to better yourself.

A lot of brothers become miserable because someone on the outside is not living up to their expectations. When a girlfriend, wife, baby mother, family member or friend shows no concern for an individual incarcerated some guys allow that to eat them up. Think about this, while you're walking around miserable do you think how you feel is affecting people on the outside? Do you think they really care whether or not you're miserable? If they did care, then they'd make sure the issues you have with them were addressed accordingly, thus limiting the amount of friction that causes your misery. Whatever is causing you such grief and misery you need to let go; being miserable takes up too much valuable energy.

When I recognized anybody I interacted with was constantly miserable I did my best to avoid them. I refused to let another's misery infect my drive to do better. You get a whole bunch of miserable people together and nothing but negativity comes out of it. Miserable people *always* stay in some sort of drama that most times pulls all those around them into it.

Miserable people never take the blame for their actions. They refuse to accept that they're the cause of their situation. The people who are constantly miserable are more then likely to be the people who need a reality check; *you caused your situation, accept that and move on*. The damage is done. Now make the conscious decision to make changes in your life instead of dwelling on the past.

You can't go anywhere in life when you're constantly miserable. You'll find yourself stuck in a world where there's no sense of peace. How does one find peace in prison? First, you have to take responsibility for your actions, your decisions, and your life. You have to look beyond what you've done and begin to look forward at what you wanna do when you get out. You have to make a conscious decision to re-invent yourself. You have to go through the necessary metamorphosis that brings about change. Once you begin to do good, you'll start to feel good. You'll begin to believe in yourself regardless if no one else does. You'll become determined to turn a bad situation into a great opportunity. You'll see a future for yourself.

Being miserable stops you from achieving any of these things. You'll have your bad days in prison which is understandable, but from experience, when you're striving to do better and you see yourself actually changing those days become less and less frequent.

The only person who can keep you down, keep you from believing in yourself, keep you from the future you deserve, and keep you from reaching the next level is YOU! Some people you know on the outside want you to spend your incarceration miserable. They don't wanna see you do better because they know if you're able to do better you might out accomplish them. Half the people you used to roll with will be doing the same things they were doing before and after you get out.

There's a strong chance during your incarceration you'll run into a staff member who's going to go out of their way to make your time as miserable as possible. You can't allow yourself to feed into that. Some prison staff are miserable too. Many of them hate what they do and feel it's their job to make your life as miserable as possible. Try to have as little contact with staff as possible. The less contact you have with staff, the better. Thinking staff is cool has led to a lot of dudes putting themselves in jams. I never joked or played with staff members. I never talked to the staff unless I had to or needed some sort of administrative assistance. When it comes to prison everything is a test and every test can somehow help prepare you for the future. If you can't stay out trouble in prison, how can you stay out of trouble back in society? If you can't duck the prison police how can you duck the real police in the streets? If you can't learn to control your anger, your stress and your attitude in prison, what are the chances that you'll be able to control these things back in society?

Exercising Patience

A friend of mine Howard "Frenchy" French always said, *"A patient man ride donkey."* One thing prison teaches you is, to be patient. Nothing happens in prison at a quickened pace. You have to wait for everything. You wait for chow, wait to see the doctor, wait for mail, for visits, to use the shower. You wait for the count to clear. You wait to move from one part of the prison to another part. You wait for almost everything. It takes patience to deal with all the waiting you endure during incarceration.

Your conditioning to deal with all the waiting begins when you're going back and forth to court before you even get sentenced to prison.

Then there's the type of patience you have to demonstrate when dealing with staff and other prisoners.

An incarcerated individual should be one of the most patient people in the world. That's why I find it amazing that after being forced to be so patient while incarcerated, some brothers go back to society and lose all sense of patience. Dudes go back to the free-world in a mad dash to do all the things they think they need to do to make up for lost time. Before you know it they're right back doing all the negative things they were doing before they went to prison.

A person should be able to exercise the same level of patience he/she has learned in prison, in society, as he/ she slowly and methodically puts all the plans he/she has into motion. To leave prison in an *"I have to make up for lost time"* mind-frame will be counter-productive to doing the right thing when you reach home. Take your time, set small goals for yourself as you move towards bigger goals. You have to pace because if you don't you'll lose all focus.

If you're willing to take the patient route it means you have your priorities in order. Going home and rushing things will have you pulling yourself in all kind of different directions. Your ability to accomplish things will be greatly diminished when you rush.

When you're released from prison people will be watching you. People will observe you to see what kind of things you're getting yourself into. If people see you running around like a chicken with his head cut off, people are gonna stay away from you. If people see you come home focused, determined with plans and the patience it takes to execute your plans, you'll be surprised what kind of doors will open for you. No matter how much you try you cannot make up for lost time. You cannot go back to society thinking that you're going to get everything you want overnight. You have to be willing to roll up your sleeves and put your work in.

In life, when you lose patience that's when everything starts going in the wrong direction. You were patient in prison so why can't you be patient when you get home? What happens is, **a brother's wants become greater than his needs**, so he gets caught up in the things he wants and forgets about surviving with only the things he needs.

In prison you get by on the things you need. So why must you rush to get so many things when you get out. You can't be influenced by what other people have to the point that it drives you to make unsound decisions in an attempt to acquire the same things. Once your wants become greater than your needs you'll find yourself willing to do almost anything except work hard to get what you want. It's going to be especially hard if you were someone who was handling large amounts of money before you went to prison. A lot of times if a dude had it going on before he went to prison, he automatically desires the same material status he once held. For some dudes to see other dudes living good, driving nice cars, wearing nice clothes or expensive jewelry drives them to have these things instantaneously.

For most of us instant gratification is what sent us to prison in the first place. Not wanting to work for the things we wanted was many brothers' shortcoming. Now, to have been through the time, to have learned what it truly means to be patient, we should have a firm grip on what it takes to be successful in society. Without the ability to be patient a newly released person from prison will be faced with many distractions, temptations, and obstacles. If you lose your sense of being patient eventually you will fall victim to those distractions and temptations. So instead of moving forward you'll move backwards. The more the distractions you allow to sidetrack you, the further backwards you'll slide.

I've seen a lot of guys return to prison during my incarceration and what I found to be the case with most of them was, all they had to account for their time on the streets was, how many women they bedded, how much weed they smoked, where the hottest clubs were, what was the latest and hippest trends. Meaningless stuff like that. No one ever returned to prison talking about how they started their own business or how they were going to school. It was always the same. You have to exercise the same level of patience you've learned while incarcerated to your life upon release.

I see no reason why you cannot achieve anything you set out to achieve in life. When we return to society we have all the necessary tools to maneuver through society successfully. Prison teaches you a lot if you're willing to adhere to the lessons that are around you. You're forced to be patient in prison, force yourself to be patient when you're released. My mother once ended a letter to me saying this, *"The race is not always won by the swift or the fastest, it is often won by the ones who can endure."*

As you travel the path of change, incorporate the learned virtue of patience to everything you do in life.

Reversing The Hustle

Reversing the hustle means taking the same energy, focus,and determination you used to do wrong, to do something constructive, productive and positive. Imagine what you could accomplish if you harnessed all the same energy; dedication, drive, and determination you used to be on top of your criminal-game and applied that to your legal hustle.

Look at the energy it takes to do wrong. Watching out for the cops, stickup kids, the schemes and so-called *game* people try to hand you on a daily basis. Trying to hide your wrong doing from everyone can get overwhelming. It's very stressful doing the wrong thing. Not knowing when the bottom is going to fall out and constantly not being able to trust people. I laugh sometimes because a lot of people didn't even know my real name until I got locked up. This is the kind of life I chose. Think how much we could accomplish if we were applying all that energy to something positive.

People automatically assume committing crime is easy. In fact it takes more energy to do wrong than it takes to do right. For example, say your hustle was drugs, people only see the end results of the money you make from selling drugs but few people see the time, the energy, and the headaches that you go through.

Let's examine the energy that goes into selling drugs. You have to do a lot of research; where to buy drugs from, who to buy drugs from, how much a certain amount of drugs cost, whether or not the person you're buying the drugs from can be trusted, what do bad drugs look like, how do you know you're getting what you paid for, will you get a money back guarantee. You have to find a place to stash the drugs, package the drugs and a place to sell the drugs. You have to enlist people to help you sell the drugs. You have to interact with the customers; you have to watch out for the police and the stickup kids. You have to buy a gun to protect your drug business, you have to be willing to use violence if needed. You have to be serious. You have to find out who your competition is, the competing prices, who's your clientele.

All of these things you have to learn and apply while doing your illegal drug hustle. There's still more you have to do. Transportation, paying workers, getting workers out of jail, and the list goes on. Again, all of these things you have to learn. You didn't wake up one day and know all of these things. You went out there after you decided to get involved in the drug trade and learned the so-called *game*.

Contrary to popular belief, there's no such thing as a *"born hustler"*. You're not born with the knowledge to sell drugs, you have to learn how to sell drugs. How good you become is another thing, but you still went through a process of learning. That's what reversing the hustle is all about, learning. Learning new things, new ways to think, new ways to acquire wealth legally, and taking that same energy you once used for negative and applying it positively.

Society wants you to believe the only kinds of hustle a person can do is illegal. Society needs you to think this way in order for you to keep coming in and out of the system. If you apply the same work ethics of your illegal hustle to a legal hustle, you have the ability to run a successful company or business endeavor.

A great deal of us already ran our own companies. The difference was, we did it illegally. We know how to do accounting, sales, marketing, expansion, takeovers, consolidating, marketing research and a host of other things that go into running a company. I said when I get back out I was going to show society exactly what I was made of and I was going to go home and represent for all the good intelligent brothers still locked down. When one of us goes home we represent all the ones we leave

148

behind because people are looking at us all in the same context. My achievements reflect positively on everyone who's locked down, not just me. If people see me doing good then they can believe that others in my situation can do good. Just as my achievements are your achievements, my failures are your failures. We hear too many stories of the brothers who go home only to come back. The stories of the brothers who go home and stay home are far and few in between. I decided prison wasn't going to be the end of my story. Instead, I was going to use the time in prison to write me a few more chapters.

When we're on the streets doing our illegal grind we were workaholics to the fifth power. Sometimes we'd stay out on the block from sun up to sun down. We didn't wanna miss a dime. When we made it big in the drug trade, we put dudes out on the strip for us, from sun up to sun down. Sometimes we'd be hustlin' so hard we wouldn't even take a shower when we finally hit the crib. We'd get a call early in the morning and be right out. We put making money in front of everything and everyone.

It just makes sense now. If you apply as much energy doing right as you applied doing wrong ,you'll succeed at whatever you choose to do. If your crime was robbing people, you had to put energy into doing that too. You had find a victim or a place to rob. You had to observe the person or place, you had to establish whether this person or place had anything of value worth robbing. You had to establish the risk involved. Whether you'd meet resistance. Whether you'd have to use violence. Whether or not you needed a weapon and if so what kind. You had to choose the proper time. You had to plan for your escape, the clothes to wear, a disguise. What to do if you were seen. All these things went into what outwardly looks like a relatively easy crime to commit.

Any criminal act takes some type of energy to commit. Committing opportunistic crimes take energy. The state of preparedness takes energy. Being ready and willing to act or react takes energy. With all this energy, anyone who goes around committing crimes could easily channel that energy into doing something positive. It's about being able to recognize that energy and use it productively, and being able to use that energy to hone your talent, skill, or ideas.

Before you launch your illegal hustle you usually start off with some sort of plan. It's the same way when you launch a legal hustle, you start off with a plan. The difference is, your legal hustle will take you a lot further and open up a lot more doors then your illegal hustle. The only doors that open for the illegal hustle are prison doors and casket doors.

So many times you hear dudes profess to be *"hustlers"* or to be *"real hustlers"*, a **REAL** hustler isn't limited to one type of hustle. He knows he can master whatever hustle he chooses. A **REAL** hustler isn't afraid or intimidated by change because he knows how to adapt and evolve. A **REAL** hustler knows the importance of having a plan that's flexible. A **REAL** hustler knows how to improvise.

If you call yourself a hustler, then being able to reverse your hustle should be easy to do, nothing to you. All the real hustlers I've run into during my incarceration were still planning and trying their hardest to make things happen even from behind the wall. Only this time they were focusing on doing it by legal means. These individuals were smart enough to recognize that the future didn't exist in crime. The future exists in making legal maneuvers with the same drive they applied doing illegal maneuvers.

Society has grown weary with crime and criminals coming out of prison only to commit more crime. Prisons have all but closed the proverbial *"revolving door"* to prisons. Society is making prisons permanent residences for people who have failed to adapt to change. Being able to leave prison nowadays is a blessing. You have to make the necessary changes in order to function when you're released.

A real hustler knows he makes the hustle, the hustle doesn't make him. All real hustlers know the so-called *game* is dead. It's a new time and a new era. Only real hustlers who know how to take what they've learned in the streets and reverse it will make it out here. The way society works today, if you're not into something positive you're in the way. Either you're gonna step up or get stepped on.

Society's hustle is to convince you the illegal hustle is the only way for you to get ahead and the only way for you to have anything of value. Society knows what your capabilities are so it makes sure it keeps you from realizing your full potential.

We only think the business world is difficult because we were never exposed to it. Society wants you to think that it's very difficult to open and run your own business, but it's not as difficult as you might think. Opening up a business is the same as opening up shop/spot to sell drugs, only you have to fill out the paper work. When you start your legal hustle, you begin by putting your plans down on paper. The principle of the hustle stays the same. Up early, first one out on the block, have the best product, treat your customers right, keep prices competitive, and do your marketing research. Look for new locations, look to expand. When you decide to reverse the hustle you put the ball back in your court and you set yourself up to win.

Staying Focused

The time you spend incarcerated is a great time to master the art of focusing. The few times a brother does leave prison with a plan, what normally happens is, once he gets back to society he loses focus. Brothers allow themselves to get sidetracked and before you know it they're all off course. Practice the art of getting and staying focused while you have the opportunity to learn new living skills. The brothers who learn how to focus while incarcerated and who take that focus to the streets are the brothers who'll have the greater chance of succeeding in the future. The most common excuse you hear when guys return to prison is how they lost their focus. That's another one of the major pitfalls brothers have when they get out, not maintaining that level of focus they had in prison.

While you're doing time you don't have nothing but time to think and get your thoughts together, things are supposed to become clearer for you. Your ability to spot and navigate around distractions should get stronger and stronger.

When I first starting writing my first book, a lot of guys were very negative and critical of me writing a urban slang language guidebook. It was really more the fact that I wanted to do something other than hangout and do nothing with them than it was about my writing. As someone who has never been a follower I continued doing what I needed to do to better me in spite of what anyone had to say. Those negative dudes I came in contact with made me wanna focus even harder on doing something positive. I looked at everyday as a day I would be moving closer to accomplishing something positive. I had no problem with believing in me.

Every successful person you've heard talk about their journey to success speaks about staying focused. You have to know what you wanna do and focus on doing that. While locked up, you'll hear all the grandiose plans dudes have for the future. Take stock of the dudes talking and you'll know right away these dudes are only talking because they can't focus in prison. How are they gonna focus on the streets? I asked this guy Whiz one time, why didn't he workout, it's not like he didn't have the time and his response was, *"I'm a join a gym when I get out."* I'm thinking, you don't work out when you have the time and you're gonna join a gym when you get out? Does that make any kind of sense to you? This was one of the main guys who used to constantly beat me over the head about all the things he was gonna do when he got out.

Listen, you can talk and talk about all the future plans you have, but if you lack the ability to focus in prison then all the stuff you talk is just talk. On the same token, if you do have plans they won't mean anything if you can't focus when you *get out* of prison. Focus takes discipline. It's something you have to be constantly aware of. Being able to spot and maneuver around distractions whenever and however they manifest themselves builds your ability to focus. Being able to stay out of situations that aren't productive or constructive builds your ability to focus.

Distractions normally come in bits and pieces. Brothers tend to think they can manage or keep the distractions under control. As your ability to focus grows, you automatically build a radar system which will alert you to things that are distractions. It's up to you to adhere to those warning signals when your radar goes off. If you ignore the warning signals or think the warning signals aren't that significant, eventually you'll lose focus because you failed to keep your guard up when the distractions come. Those little distractions become full blown problems and by then it's too late because you're already off your original course

I say that to say this, you must maintain a strong level of focus. Get yourself straight first and all the other stuff will come. If you learn to maintain focus when you make it back to society you'll always be conscious of the ramifications of doing wrong. Staying focused keeps you in tune with the real risks and dangers of living a street life.

There are many distractions back in society. A lot of the distractions one might encounter come from his/her surroundings. When a dude gets out and returns to the old neighborhood, to the old friends with the same old habits (like hanging out, smoking marijuana, and/or drinking) if he hasn't learned how to focus while he's away it's going to be extremely hard for him to get focused with all the old negativity surrounding him. Not saying that it can't be done, but you have to be strong, that much more determined and focused.

If possible, go live somewhere brand new to you upon your release from prison. Live somewhere where you don't know anyone and no one knows you. Once you make the conscious decision to make changes in your life you have to cut ties to the old way, friends, and habits. You have to start fresh. Give yourself a chance to start life over in a new environment, you'll find it much easier to focus on your goals and plans.

Keep in mind that changing your ways and coming home with a plan is only part of the puzzle. Other parts of the puzzle consist of staying focused, remaining humble and weathering the storms of distraction and temptation. There will be trying times when you get out, situations will arise that you didn't plan for and you'll have to improvise, adjust and readjust to them. These will be the times that'll test you. I have had some set backs since coming home, but each set back further fueled my determination to succeed. I refuse to lose. Plans are meant to be flexible. As long as you don't stray away from the plan you can always accomplish what you set out to accomplish.

Learning how to focus is just half the battle, staying focused is the other half. The average person on the street who's never been to prison finds it hard to focus and doesn't have the necessary time it takes to learn how to focus.

Learning to Appreciate

There are so many lessons to be learned during one's incarceration. Learning how to appreciate is another major lesson to be learned and to be lived by. When you're ripping and running in the streets you tend to take a lot of things for granted. It's only when you're taken away from those things and those things are no longer available to you, you realize what you've lost, thrown away, or neglected. Many times we take people for granted. Not taking into full consideration how our actions affect others. One of the worst things we take for granted is our freedom. We walk around with this misconception that we can get away with crime or that we're smart enough not to get caught without even realizing this is the way things are set up for us to think. To make us think we can get over.

As you go through your incarceration you should take full stock of all the things you should be appreciative of. Being alive. Your health. The people in your corner. Communication with your children. Your mother and/or father.

Having someone constantly telling you what you can and cannot do and always watching your every move should teach you how to appreciate having control over your life. Once you have your freedom taken away from you one time, your appreciation for your freedom is supposed to be something you never take for granted again.

To have gone through your incarceration and not learn appreciation, is the same as going through life without ever learning what's important to you. If you're unable to learn these life's lessons during your incarceration, you're bound to repeat the same mistakes over and over again until one day you'll wake up an old and basically useless soul. No use to yourself because you've squandered so much of your life away and no good to anyone else because you haven't accumulated anything of value or substance.

Learning how to appreciate comes from recognizing your situation, no matter how grave, could've been worse. It's also about being conscious that there is always someone in a worse situation then you're in. Learn how to appreciate the simple things life has to offer.

So many brothers fail to appreciate having complete control over their own life. They go right back to society and do the same things they were doing before coming to prison. Once you learn how to appreciate things like your freedom, make it a constant goal to never have your freedom taken away. Show the people who've stuck by you appreciation by going back to society and doing the right thing. Live by the changes you've made over the years. Show them the time and support they've invested in you wasn't in vain. That their support was for a worthy cause.

When you learn how to appreciate things, you hold those things dear to your heart. You wake up everyday with appreciation.

Moving Fast Going Nowhere

I want you to observe something and hopefully what I'm pointing out to you makes sense. Watch dudes when it's time to go to recreation, when it's time to go to chow, time to go on a visit, or when they're trying to meet up with their homies. Watch how fast these dudes be moving. Isn't it funny how fast dudes be moving in prison, not to be going anywhere. Now watch a dude on his release day and I bet you he doesn't move nowhere as fast as he was when he was jetting throughout the prison. I used to watch some dudes the day they were getting released and you could see the uncertainty written on their faces. I used to ask dudes going home what they were gonna do when they get home and a lot of times dudes would say, "I have to see when I get out there." You can't leave prison thinking like that and expect to succeed out here. You not only have to have a plan A, you better have a plan B, C, D, E, and the rest of the alphabet.

When dudes asked me what I was gonna do when I got out I had several things to tell them. I know most of them didn't believe I would do any of the things I was talking about but I BELIEVED! And that's all that mattered. Dudes used to clown me when I'd try to tell them about getting out here and doing the right thing. This kid from Jersey named Smiley even called me an oddball. What he didn't understand was, there's nothing wrong with being an oddball. I took that as a compliment because that means I'm different from everyone else. I used to laugh. Few brothers understand, that in order to be a leader you have to be different, think different and want different. Stepping away from the pack is nothing new for brothers like me, so remarks like that never bothered me.

Words of Encouragement

Gentlemen and ladies I wouldn't tell any one of y'all something wrong or something I'm not willing to stand on myself. I *wish* I had someone to give me the kind of jewels that I'm giving you in this book, when I was doing my bid. I had thirteen and a half long years to learn the lessons that I'm schooling you on and it wasn't always easy. I had my share of a drama while I was away but I learned from each situation. The times I did find myself in drama, it was always behind someone else's foolishness. You have some dudes who aren't happy unless they're in some nonsense or causing some nonsense. You know the saying, *"misery likes company."* Nothing is truer in prison.

When I write brothers on lock-down I always encourage them to come out here with a plan. I'm setting up a media company to self-publish this book and my next book titled **Once Upon A Time in** Brooklyn. **I have two documentary projects waiting in the** wings, plus I wanna help guys on lock-down get their work published. A lot of these fly by night publishing companies are taking advantage of dudes with these poor book deals. They know all a dude wanna do is get his book published and out on the streets and they're capitalizing off of that. I wanna set something up so a brother will have an opportunity to have something when he gets out.

I can't stress to you enough about the importance of coming home with a workable plan. Without one you're destined to fail out here. Even with a plan, you have to persevere. Things don't just pop-off overnight and you have to be willing to see your plans through no matter the struggle or sacrifice. I get frustrated sometimes because I want or feel things should be going a certain way just because I'm doing something positive. My man Danny keeps reminding me that all I'm doing right now is planting the seeds and in order for those seeds to grow I must be patient and time must pass. That's where the frustration comes in because I want things to happen faster. This is the critical time period where a lot of brothers make hasty decisions. I'm staying the course because I have to. A lot is riding on the seeds I plant today. People expect me to fail because they see so many other brothers come home and fail. I want you to join me in my plight to prove them wrong. Feel me?

Incarceration has been so stigmatized in society, that people almost expect you to go back to prison after a while. You hear too many stories about the dudes who come home for a few months and end up going back. With all the time brothers spend away, we should be coming out here with a focus that people should be respecting. When you're away you have so much time to think, to plan, to grow. If dudes applied themselves in a positive way they could come home accomplishing great things.

With me it was a no brainer... I knew I didn't wanna go back to prison. Now the question was, what was I gonna do to make sure that I didn't? Change. Change my way of thinking, my perspective, my attitude. Change my priorities.

Everybody deals with incarceration differently and no matter how you choose to deal with it everything you're going through I went through too. That's why I'm tellin' you what's really good. I hope I can tell you these things without them going in one ear and out the other. I love my brothers to death but if my brothers come home on the same ol' same ol' they were on before incarceration, I'm staying as far away from my brothers as possible. I refuse to let my brothers jeopardize my freedom. I haven't come this far to go backwards. I'm out here trying to build something positive and I'll be darn if I'm going to throw away my plans or my freedom. We're not youngsters anymore. I'm not goin' out like one of these so-called O.G.'s who don't have anything tangible to show for their lives on this earth but a bunch of back in the days war stories. That's not the kind of future I have planned for myself.

Close All Open Cases

It's extremely important to clear up any open cases you may have while you're incarcerated. If you don't, you may find yourself unable to get out of prison once your sentence on this case is complete. It happened to me even though I was trying to close all open cases over the years.

New York placed a detainer on me 10 days before my release from Federal custody. In 1991 I had jetted on a 1 1/2 to 3 in the state, and the state wanted me to do that time. The day my Fed sentence ended I was arrested by New Jersey authorities (being the institution I was being released from was in New Jersey) on a fugitive warrant issued by New York. I was taken to this desolate county jail in New Jersey pending my extradition to New York. While in New Jersey I had an extradition hearing on the outstanding warrant in New York. On advice from the lawyers my mom had gotten me, instead of letting New York come get me and bring me back to New York, she paid for bounty hunters to escort me back to New York on the terms that I immediately turn myself in at Brooklyn Supreme Court.

When I got to court I was remanded to Rikers Island for 12 days. Those two weeks on Rikers Island were more then enough to reassure my conviction to stay out of prison. Those were the worst two weeks in jail I had spent in my whole life. The conditions were nothing short of barbaric. I mean I been to the Island back in the days and I know it's not the best jail in the country, but the conditions are a hundred times worse now. I was so disgusted that I was ready to cop out to the 1 1/2 to 3 just to get shipped upstate.

Luckily the two lawyers mom had gotten me were thorough. The judge was fair and I had my business together. Not only did I have legal grounds to stand on (I had been contacting the prosecutor's office during my incarceration and they failed to respond), I was able to show the court how I had spent the years positively. When I got back to court the Judge gave me a dollar bail. So after 13 years, 6 months and 2 days I finally got a chance to taste freedom again.

I didn't even know how to use a metro card when I was released from Rikers Island. I was bugging when I saw everybody walking around talking on cell phones. It only took me a couple days to get my bearings. After two weeks on the streets I was working and I was laying the foundation for all the things I had planned. You can get used to freedom again real fast. It hits me sometimes when I do something as simple as going in the refrigerator or talking on the phone longer than 15 minutes. It's easy to forget once you get into a steady grind, then you always find things that keep you from forgetting. Those are the things that keep you mindful of how fragile freedom is.

After going back and forth to court for two months, the case was dismissed for lack of due diligence on behalf of the prosecutor's office; for failing to respond to my repeated attempts to have this matter taken care of when they were aware of my whereabouts. That means, the felony was erased from my record as well.

Do everything within your power to clear up any outstanding cases you might have. You don't want your future put on hold because something from your past pops up.

Pride, Principles & Values

One of the things that I have working for me is, I was able to cut loose all the phony street pride, principles, and values I used to live by in the past. I don't get caught up in how things look or supposed to go in the street anymore.

In prison and in the streets, we often live by all these so- called principles, principles that'll make a man beat, stab, or kill another man over something petty. Principles that have us out there selling drugs, robbing people, shooting people, and God knows what else, yet we don't possess enough principles to work a minimal job that can help keep us out of prison. That doesn't make any sense. Why can't we have the same strong convictions we have in prison and street life, in the legitimate world?

It's that misguided pride which keeps a brother from working a minimal wage job when he first comes home, but when he's away he has to work for pennies a day. You can work for pennies a day in prison but you can't work for pennies in society when you're free? It's that kind of misguided pride that keep brothers stagnant.

Where's the principles when dudes are regularly belittled, humiliated, disrespected and sometimes assaulted by correctional staff....? Yet will curse an employer out if he feels the employer is giving him a hard time. If you can build up a high tolerance for the negativity that goes on in prison then you can come out here with the same high tolerance level. Just like in prison, in the legitimate world you'll also come across people who'll go out their way to push your buttons.

After enduring all I had to endure while incarcerated, I don't have the same kind of hang-ups anymore. I don't allow things to bother me like I used to. How could I when I had people telling me when to eat, sleep, and sometimes when to bathe? I've come across a couple minor situations since being released, but each time I've kept cool and handled those situations with finesse.

One thing that doesn't change whether you're a street dude, whether you're just coming home from prison or you're just a normal nine-to-five Joe, life is and will always be a *thinking mans game.* If you can think before you act or react, you'll go a lot further and accomplish a lot more in life. To think is to rationalize, to weigh out the pros and cons, the benefits versus the consequences.

Every man should have principles, but it's the type of principles he has that tell the true character of the man. Most brothers don't want their sons or daughters living by the same misguided principles they lived by on the streets. We know, whether we want to admit it or not, that this system of street pride, jail/street principles, criminal/ prison codes of conduct and values, are worthless.

Street pride means nothing when you don't have the respect of your mother, your kids and other people who know what you're really capable of. Don't let foolish street pride *(keepin' it real/'hood)* hinder you from reaching your goals out here. We shortchange ourselves so much by believing in these misguided ways of living.

We put so much value in the wrong things, like money. We value money so much we're willing to die for it, kill another over it, or go to prison because of it. We put too much value in materialistic living. We value how we look over how we live. In the streets it's all about the image of success as opposed to being successful. We have to get away from this phony value system that we've fallen victim to. It's more than about time that we adopted new and positive values.

Adopting new values, principles & pride

How does one adopt new values, principles and pride after believing in such a misguided system for so long? Easy. Make a list of all your values and principles, then examine them. Example, if someone bumps into you without saying excuse me, do you say something, keep it movin', or do you go into combat mode?

Make a list of the benefits and the consequences of your values and principles. Make a list of people who may share your values and principles (and if most the people you come up with are criminals, whether fictional or real, living or dead, that'll speak for itself). Evaluate the people who have tried to teach you positive values and principles when you were younger; your moms, grand moms, aunt, uncle, a teacher, or an older adult. Then analyze which values and principles worked for you and which worked against you. Then you'll figure out which values and principles you'll wanna retain and which ones you need to drop like a bad habit.

My mom raised me with some darn good values and principles. The streets are what got me all turned around. When I went through the stage of re-evaluating my values and principles I was able to reflect on the values and principles that were first embedded in me from early childhood. Starting from that early period in my life I began to re-program myself.

The large majority of brothers come from an early home environment that emphasized good values and principles. A great number of brothers I've run into in the system will tell you, *"I come from a good family"* or *"my moms didn't raise me like this"* or *"I didn't have to go the street route."*

People act like every brother who's been to prison or who's been in trouble grew up a bona fide criminal. When I run into people who thought they knew me, they always ask me, *"how did you of all people write a book?"* Before a lot of brothers got lost in the street life most had promising futures. It's the nonsense that we picked up in the streets that had us running around like we weren't taught or brought up any better. It's time to let go of those misguided morals and principles.

You adopt new pride when you truly feel good about the way you're living now. You feel pride knowing that you have changed for the better. When you're out here working, sacrificing and struggling to put your plans together, you feel proud of yourself because you know how easily it is to fall back into the same negative behavior. Change is something to feel very good about, because not everyone can change. Some people change for a while but wind up succumbing to the temptation of their old ways and go right back into negativity. I take pride in knowing that I had the strength and courage to change.

Too many of us can't seem to put that phony street pride in the trash can of the past. Brothers have too much street pride to work in McDonalds, wash dishes, or clean toilets (which a lot of did in prison), but not enough pride to stop from asking another man for five or ten dollars. Dudes always complaining about not being able to find work when they get out, but the thing is, where there are jobs available dudes don't wanna do that kind of work. There are jobs out here.

Street pride will have you thinking you're too good or big of a man to work for minimum wage. Real pride makes you feel like a man because you can work for minimum wage to get you where you want to go in life.

Laws and Penalties

If everything I've said isn't enough to encourage you to change, think about all the messed up laws that have been placed on the books in the last decade and a half. During the many years I spent in the Federal system, I've heard some of the craziest stories pertaining to cases that brothers were in prison for. When it comes to the Federal justice system it doesn't take a lot to send you to prison. All it takes is a couple of people to get together and say that you supplied them with drugs and you can pretty much go to prison. This is called the conspiracy law.

Conspiracy is defined as such: *a secret plan by a group to do something unlawful or harmful.*

The conspiracy law basically says that you commit a crime when you *'conspire'* to commit a crime regardless if that crime was carried out or not. When you speak about or plan a crime with someone you commit conspiracy. I know a lot of brothers who've gone down because of a conspiracy drug charge. In a conspiracy drug case, there doesn't have to be any drugs physically confiscated. The statements from an informant and/or cooperating co- defendant can send you to prison for a long, long time. I know instances where brothers have gotten life sentences based on the statements and testimony of others.

When it comes to sentencing you for a conspiracy drug charge, that's another thing. The Feds calculate your time based on the federal guidelines which take in account factors like your role in the offense, your prior criminal history and the amount of drugs alleged in the conspiracy. When there's no drugs actually confiscated in the conspiracy the court will sentence you based on a guess-stimation of the drugs supposedly involved.

I know this Jamaican kid right now named Capone who was sentenced to life for a drug conspiracy in N.C. and there were no drugs actually confiscated in his case. He went to trial and people testified that he gave them an ounce or two of crack-cocaine once a week for six months. The prosecutor said okay, and calculated 2 ounces of crack cocaine once a week for six months and that equaled 48 ounces over the course of six months. Then they said he was the leader/boss, so the prosecutor boosted his sentence for his leadership role. When he was found guilty at trial, the judge gave him a life sentence. Even if the judge thought the sentence was too harsh and wanted to give him a lighter sentence he couldn't because he was bound by the Federal sentencing Guidelines.

I know a brother who got twenty years for telling an informant he could sell him a couple guns. The dude couldn't really get the guns and had no intentions of getting the guns, yet the dude still wound up with 20 years because he allegedly *conspired* to sell the informant the guns.

Back in the days we used to think we'd be safe if we weren't caught WITH the drugs or if we didn't get caught WITH the gun. We thought we couldn't go to jail. That ain't the way it works these days.

For those of us who've been through the system, we supposed to be more conscious then everyone else when it comes to the laws. We get to witness firsthand the lopsidedness of the laws, yet dudes get out of prison and forget.

The State criminal justice system is just as twisted as the Feds. The Federal government forced the states to enact all these 'Truth in Sentencing Reforms' in the nineties. In order to receive federal funding the states went bananas with the sentencing reform schemes. States followed suit and enacted sentencing schemes which called for people to do 85% of their sentence. The Feds took sentencing overhaul to a whole new level when it abolished all forms of parole for Federal prisoners.

Now when you get 15 years like I got, you're doing 85% of that 15 years day for day. Which in turn means you do thirteen and a half years straight.

I've seen first times offenders get ten, fifteen, twenty years and sometimes life in prison for getting caught up in a drug conspiracy. A Federal conspiracy is one of the hardest cases to beat because it comes down to your word or the word of someone who is cooperating with the government. The Feds have a 98 percent conviction rate.

I know a couple brothers doing time right now because their words were misinterpreted by the Feds who were investigating someone they knew. All you have to do is call someone who's under investigation by the Feds and you could very well find yourself part of that investigation too. Brothers are in prison today because they introduced two people and those two people would go on later to commit a crime. You can go to prison for *having knowledge* of a crime. Socializing with people who were being investigated by the Feds can get you caught up in a conspiracy investigation. And these are just a few examples of how easy it is to go to jail nowadays.

We have to admit to ourselves that we're pretty much out of our league when it comes to indulging in criminal activity. How can we expect to be successful criminals when our criminal resource capacity is nothing compared to the crime fighting resources of local, state, and federal law enforcement. Stop to think..... These people can go anywhere in the world to investigate or arrest a criminal, so what's going to stop them from snatching up a lowly street hustler. When these people want you, you're just as good as caught.

Every time I thought I heard the most incredible federal conspiracy story, I would hear another story that would leave me dumbfounded. I know sons who have told on fathers, brothers who have told on brothers, and dudes who have told on women or their baby's mom. Every shocking story and every twisted ending to a case reinforced my conviction to get away from this whole criminal environment.

If there was ever such a thing as honor among criminals, that concept is no longer respected among the greater majority of people committing crime. The times have changed drastically and I pray to God that brothers currently on lock-down can change with them.

I Hated Prison

I can't speak for the next man, but I hated being incarcerated. I hated people having power over me. Telling me what to do, what I couldn't do, when to eat, when to sleep. I hated subjecting my mother to the disrespect some prison staff show our people when they came to visit us. I hated not being treated with a little amount of decency. I hated not getting the proper medical attention when I needed it. I hated seeing brothers die because they didn't get the proper medical attention. I hated having 15 minutes to talk to my loved ones on the phone. My man Pop from Philly put it best one day when he said, *"all we are is phone fathers."* I hated being a phone father. You can't possibly raise a kid over the phone.

I hated prison staff going through my personal belongings. I hated when brothers would be ready to kill each other over something dumb, yet would cower when disrespected by staff. I hated having no rights. I hated being in a position where my life was in someone else's hands.

Here's something to consider, there's a law on the books that literally says, *"in the event of a war breaking out in this country, all prisoners can be executed."* The thinking behind that is, if war was to breakout in this country prisoners would be a threat because they would wanna fight the government. That's deep. There were many times I'd lay in my bunk at night and imagine the prison staff sending poisonous gas through the vents and killing us all.

I hated eating the same garbage food. I hated prison staff reading my mail, when it came in and as it was going out. You couldn't even seal a letter when you put it the mailbox. I hated seeing my kids growing up in pictures. I hated not being there for my mother when she needed me. I hated not being there for my brother when he was sick.

With so many reasons to hate prison, there was no way I was gonna put myself back in the same situation again. Brothers complain about being locked up everyday all day while they're there, but when they get a chance to run the streets again their hatred for prison life fades away. That's crazy! I hated being incarcerated, so I know I don't wanna go through that experience ever again. Commonsense tells me to stay out of prison, you have to do this, this and this. To stay out of prison you don't do that, that and that. It's really that simple. If I used to smoke marijuana before I went away and I know smoking marijuana can send me back to prison, without a doubt I wouldn't smoke marijuana. I wouldn't wanna test positive for marijuana therefore causing my supervised release to be revoked, thus sending me back to prison.

It's all a matter of the choices you make that'll keep you from going back to prison. I don't care how slick or game tight you think you are, you can't and won't make it out here if you don't make some real changes in your life.

Obligation To Change

We have a real obligation to make these changes while incarcerated because a lot of us are to blame for the condition our neighborhoods are in today. We were major contributors to the chaos, mayhem and destruction that have plagued our communities. When we were out there committing our crimes we never understood the affect and influence that we'd have over the younger generation. We never stopped to think that a generation of young people would grow up, die and go to prison thinking the only way to make money was to make it illegally in the streets.

Young people watched us, looked up to us and when we came through wearing the fly clothes, the expensive jewelry and driving the latest cars they idolized us. They grew up imitating the images of the supposedly successful street dude. A lot of them would walk in those same street shoes as they became young adults.

We are obligated to get out here and school the younger generation. Young people don't have a clue what's facing them when they're out there in the streets. Young people these days are out of control. They buy into all the false illusions of street life and think that's all there is to life. The saddest thing you can see while incarcerated, is a youngster young enough to be your son walk through the doors.

We have to change in order to stop that from being the norm. Without our guidance, our sons and daughters are growing up with no direction. While we're away we have to change for them, no matter how hard it might be to reach the younger generation it's our obligation and duty to educate them. To school them about how the streets hold nothing positive for them. The only way we can expect to reach them is being living examples of positive change.

We even made going to jail or prison cool. We called and wrote the 'hood and bragged about how we were running things in jail or prison and eventually made jail and prison an extension of the streets. We sent home pictures that reflected how good we were doing in jail or prison. When we came home from prison we dazzled young people with our prison stories, and young people ate that nonsense up.

Dudes like us have had a lot of influence on the streets, even if that influence was negative. Now imagine the good we could do if we decided to influence young people positively. If we would flip the script and teach youngsters that the streets aren't cool, that going to jail isn't cool, that hustling isn't cool, that killing your own kind isn't cool. We can teach them that beefs don't have to be dealt with violently. That using or selling drugs isn't cool. I'm sure that we'd have an impact on young people because we are the same dudes youngsters used to get their cues from. If all we show young people is the negative side of life, then that's what they're gonna gravitate towards.

Young people have it hard out here trying to navigate through life. They're constantly being bombarded with all these negative images. For instance, all these urban so- called street magazines do nothing but promote negativity. Every feature article is about a drug dealer or some violent drug gang. These magazines do nothing to uplift young people. That's why it's important that brothers like us start to fight back and tell the youth that what they're being fed about the streets is rotten to the core. That there's nothing glamorous about street life.

Dudes like us, we're the ones who created the atmosphere for hip-hop and urban culture to be what it is today when it was just in its infancy. The hip-hop culture today is not the hip-hop culture we created. It's been turned into something that has been more destructive to the community than uplifting of it. People have used our lives and stories to exploit and perpetuate what street life is through rap music.

Being we're the same brothers who contributed to the destruction, chaos and mayhem within our communities, we should be the same brothers who contribute to the cleaning and up lifting of them. In a collective act of redemption brothers have to start setting positive examples for our young people to follow. We have to start tearing down those false images of what cool and gangsta is, for starters. A movement like this doesn't happen overnight or take shape easily. The movement starts with each one of us, when each one of us starts taking responsibility to change our ways. I'm out here and I see the damage we have done. It's nothing to feel proud of.

When this book comes out I plan to hookup with some youth organizations and hit the speaking circuit talking to young people who are at risk of going to prison behind street life. Hopefully I'll be able to use my experiences as a deterrent to young people who think going to prison is cool. It's a need for that out here. Plus it's good to have motivational speaking in your resume when it comes to skills that you have.

Finding A Purpose in Life

I left a lot of good brothers behind. Brothers who may never be coming home. I would always tell these brothers even though they're faced with such a fate they still have a purpose in this life. And it's true, because everyone on this earth has a purpose. It's up to that individual to find what that purpose is. In the gravest of circumstances you can find something that gives you purpose. I would always tell these brothers their purpose was to preach staying out of prison to all the brothers who'll be going home.

Brothers doing sentences ranging from 25 years to100 years to life have a certain level of respect in prison. If they got together and began to condemn all the negativity goin' on in prison and goin' on in the streets brothers would definitely follow suit. If brothers in prison on a whole started promoting positive change, do you know how great of an impact they'd have? Not only in prison but on the streets as well. Prison and the streets are intertwined greatly.

I'm out here doing my part. I came home to show people that there are brothers coming home to handle their business. I wanna kill that perception which suggests every brother in prison is no good, won't amount to anything or will eventually go back. I'm trying to set an example that brothers can follow and people can respect. An example that offers hope to so many brothers who need to change their game plan altogether before it's too late.

8 Million Stories

There's an old saying that goes, "there's 8 million stories in this naked city..." Everyone has a story, everyone's life is a story. I always encourage brothers to write their story. Why not, use the time you have to document your life. If not for the purpose of one day having your story published, do it as a means to better learn about yourself. I've found writing in general can be a form of therapy and writing about your life can be a way to heal yourself.

Brothers who have come up the way we have, been through what we've been through and seen the things that we've seen, have extremely interesting stories to tell. What would make your story even more fantastic would be the journey you traveled in order to better yourself. How you were able to turn a negative situation into a positive opportunity. People want and need to hear stories about brothers like us who've overcome insurmountable odds and won.

The book industry is crazy out here. I attended the Harlem Book Fair for the first time during the summer, and I'm here to tell you, African American's are writing more than any time in history. There were black authors and black publishers all over the place for two whole blocks. It was a beautiful feeling to be surrounded by so much positivity. People came out and were very supportive of the writers and it was something.

Nowadays it's so easy to get a book published. You can do everything yourself. From the writing to the publishing and everything in-between. Printing, editing, marketing, promoting and the part I love the best, the selling. Whether you write your life story, someone else's story, or hell, a prison cookbook, there's something you're very knowledgeable about that you can turn into a book. People read. They like to read about everything under the sun. I encourage you to write. You have the time. Writing has given lots of brothers a second chance they'd been striving for.

Time Management

How you manage your time out here is extremely important and can determine how much you achieve and how long it takes. Time in society isn't the same as time in prison. In prison you live in an structured time environment. From the time you wake up in the morning to the time you go to bed you basically have your time managed for you. Out here you have to manage your time in a way that every moment is spent doing something meaningful or constructive.

If you use the concept of structured time management in the streets you'll find your time will be used much more efficiently. In prison you're given a specific amount of time to get from one place to another so you prepare ahead of time to get there between that window of movement. Do the same thing on the street when you have places to go, leave early giving yourself ample time to arrive on time.

In prison you plan your day or days ahead of time in order to use your time efficiently. When you're locked down most dudes don't wake up in the morning wondering what they're going to do today, they already know. You know you're only working within a limited amount of time to do what you want or need to do, so you already have your day mapped out. A lot of brothers keep schedules for their days. Do the same thing on the streets. This keeps you in tune to how you're using your time. In most prisons its mandatory that you get up early, go to eat and then go to work. It's the same concept in the streets. Up early, eat and head to work.

Time management is also about priorities. No matter what your plans are when you come home, you're gonna have to earn a living too. You might not be able to spend the time you thought you were gonna spend implementing your plan because working and earning a living takes priority over everything. This is where your ability to focus comes in. While you're working try to fit time in during your day to work on some aspect of your plan. When you reach home after work, use the evenings to work on your plan. Weekends should be spent working toward your plan as well.

Time management is also about sacrifice. You can either spend your time going out partying and chasing women or you can use every moment available laying the foundation of your future plans. 2006 was the first full summer I've seen on the streets since 1991 and all I did this summer was work, work, and work. When I wasn't working I was working on my projects, I didn't go to one cookout, amusement park, or pool party. The only thing I did do, was take my mom to dinners and attend the Harlem book fair which was goal oriented. I sacrificed all the fun I could have had this summer for the sake of continuing to implement my goals. This way when next summer rolls around I can enjoy the fruits of my labor.

Building a Support System

Even though we like to believe we can do everything on our own, we all need some form of help sometime from somebody. If you have a strong support system in your corner upon your release it will help make your transition from prison a lot smoother than if you're going at it alone.

A support system is a group of people who are there to help you put the pieces to your life back together. Your support system helps prop you up until you're able to stand on your own feet. It's not suppose to take care of you. Each person in your support system can serve a useful purpose, from lending you a ear to possibly lending you money for carfare, getting your necessary documents, etc.

Building a strong support system while in prison can be difficult but it is a very important piece of putting together your new game plan. You can start building your system by reaching to your family, closest friends and then expand accordingly. Eventually you want to include people who share similar experiences as you so have people who can relate to your challenges.

In the process of building your support system you may have to repair broken relationships with family and friends you burned bridges with prior to your incarceration. You have to be prepared for possible initial resistance to your efforts of reconciliation because you have lost people's trust. So the first order of business is trying to rebuild trust with the people you hurt. In order to have a strong support system, people have to be able to trust you. The only way you can get people to trust you again is by showing them you have changed.

You want positive people in your support system, people you can go to when you are feeling overwhelmed and discouraged. People who will talk you through a tough situation or guide you as you find your way after prison. People in your support system night be able to help you find a job, housing or point you to resources that help you with your immediate needs. When you don't want to do is become a burden on your support system, so remember they are there to help you not take care of you.

Incarcerated On Paper

Incarcerated on paper means being on parole, probation or some sort of court ordered supervision (usually following your incarceration). In order to avoid running afoul of your supervision conditions it's best to know exactly what is expected of you as soon as you meet with your parole officer. Keep in mind you're still incarcerated you're just not surrounded by barbwire and fences, so follow all your conditions to the letter.

There's nothing wrong with trying to establish a good relationship with your parole or probation officer. It's counter productive to see your p.o. as the enemy when their job is too make sure you meet your supervision conditions. Most people tend to blame their p.o. for violating their parole, instead of looking at the reasons they gave the p.o. to violate them. In some cases you might run into a p.o. who seems extremely hard on his/her clients and looking for any little things to send them back to prison on a violation, understanding that, it is your job to make sure you don't give your p.o. a reason to violate you.

If you need to travel, you ask for permission. You need to move, you notify your p.o. you moved. You have programs to report to, report. You have to get a job, provide the p.o. with a paper trail of your job searches. You have a curfew, meet your curfew. If you follow the conditions that have been set for you, then you leave no reasons for violation. Having a problem or foreseeable problem with a spouse, girlfriend/boyfriend, baby momma or baby father talk to your p.o. about it in advance, don't wait until a situation escalates and explodes and then try to explain your side of the story, may be too late then. Get out in front of all possible situations as you see them unfolding. Like it or not, your p.o. holds the keys to your freedom in his/her hands. You can establish a good relationship with your p.o. by sharing and following through with your plans.

Show your p.o. you're serious about building a positive life yourself and 9 time out of 10 he/she will support you. In that 1 remaining case, it's still up to you to follow through with your plans and don't give your p.o. a reason to violate you. P.O's love clients who don't give them any headaches, it makes their job easier. If you become a headache for your p.o. eventually he/she will find a way and a reason to shut you down.

Things to Do Immediately

One of the first things you wanna do upon your release is obtain identification. This is extremely important because everything you do from seeking a job to opening a banking account will require an ID. In most cases the only kind of ID that is acceptable is a state issued ID. Even if you sign up for public assistance you'll need ID

If you don't have a birth certificate you can go to The Bureau of Vital Records (in New York City it's located at 40 Worth Street across from 26 Federal Plaza). Bring your prison ID, release papers, and your Social Security card if you have one (some prisons will help you get your SSC before your release). You'll have to pay a filing fee.

If you don't have your Social Security Card, you have to go to a social security office with a letter from your P.O. stating who you are, your date of birth and bring your prison release papers and social security will issue you your social security card.

You'll need your birth certificate, your social security card, and your prison ID/release papers when you go to motor vehicles to get your state issued ID, your driving permit and/or your driver's license.

Once you have your identification in order, you're ready to hit the pavement looking for employment (keep all your options open and contact some of the organizations that I have provided info on).

If you don't have a steady address, rent a p.o. box or mail drop with a street address. You'll have enough ID now to meet the rental requirement. Have all your bills and such go to this address.

Getting On Your Feet

Here's a few quick job related opportunities to get you on your feet as soon as you come home. As soon as you hit the streets get a messenger job, learn the city. While doing the messenger thing get your driving business in order. Pay any old tickets and things like that and get your license as soon as possible. With a drivers license you can get a driving job just like that. If you buy a used mini van, slap some commercial plates on it, I guarantee you'll get a job driving for a messenger/courier service. Messenger and courier services are always in need of drivers with their own vans. You can walk into any messenger/courier company and get a job just like that, when you have your own van with commercial plates on it.

You can make several hundred dollars a week. In some places drivers are averaging eight hundred to a thousand dollars a week depending on how busy the company is. With the van you can do odd moving jobs on the side too.

There's a web site called craigslist.org you can go to, where lots of people go to post inquiries when in need of moving help.

If you have a van you can do independent contract for cable companies like Direct TV, Dish Network and Cablevision. These companies hire sub-contractors for installation and maintenance. If you have a van they'll hire and train you. Visit the parent company's web site and inquire about being an independent installation contractor.

You can go to places like Home Depot or Ikea on the weekend and post up for people who need rides. You can make contact with people or organizations that organize street fairs and let then know you're available to pickup and drop off vendors. You can make a nice amount of money picking up vendors on the weekend. People will

take your number and refer to other people and before you know it people will be calling you left and right.

Having a driver's licence is extremely important out here. It's your instant meal ticket. If you don't want to do the messenger thing, there's lots of other jobs out here that want drivers. You can drive corporate cars/limos after having your license for six months. I used to think you had to have a special license or endorsement, but that's not the case. All you have to do is pass a drug screening to get your certificate to drive corporate limos.

Then there's always companies looking to hire dudes with their CDL license and some will even send you to school for you to get your CDL. Having a license out here is like having a platinum Master Card. You'll always be able to eat.

There's a high demand for movers. Again, if you go to craigslist.org there's always a listing under labor, where moving companies are looking for movers.

Look into what job opportunities are available in civil services sectors in your city, ie. Sanitation, parks department, transit authority. In New York City you can get certain city jobs with 1 felony or 4 felonies, you just have to be honest when disclosing everything you've been convicted of. I know people who've been in state prison, been convicted of violent crimes and they work for transit right now. It's all about being honest when you fill out the paperwork. Take city tests while you're out there rebuilding your life.

Establishing Credit

If you've never established or have messed up your credit I can't stress to you enough the importance of having good credit out here. Some jobs and almost all landlords run credit checks on people. Even some women might wanna do a credit check on you. People use credit as a way to get a picture of the type of person you are. If you have poor credit, a lot of times people will look at you as being irresponsible because you didn't keep your bills paid. And visa versa, good credit reflects positively on you and people see you can pay your bills on time.

Here's some simple steps you can take to get you on the road to establishing a credit history.

Open a checking account with the first check you receive from your new job and deposit all your earnings for the next six weeks thereafter. Your bank will have a secured credit card plan that you wanna apply for after six weeks of depositing your earned income. A secured credit card only allows you to spend the amount on the card, but it's still accepted as a credit card everywhere you go. Put a minimum of 300 dollars on it. When you get the secured credit card, use it, but only pay a little over the minimum payment required each month to help establish your credit history. After making 4-6 payments on your secured credit card, apply for an instant credit card/account at any department store. You can walk right up to the cashier and fill out the application right there. After 8 months of using both your secured credit card and your store credit card, you can then go to your bank and apply for a regular credit card.

Using these steps, you should be able to make a major credit purchase after 6-8 months. You can go to the bank and take out a small auto loan for the van you need to drive for a courier company.

The thing about establishing credit is, YOU HAVE TO PAY YOUR BILLS ON TIME! You have to create a track record of being able to pay your bills. If you can do this after about 18 months your credit should be good enough for you to consider purchasing yourself a piece of property. There's so many programs out here that'll help put you in a house, condo or coop as long as your credit is good.

Most of us never established credit so we're in a good position to create a strong credit score for ourselves.

Journey of Change

by Contributing Authors

J.M. Benjamin

Storm Weeks Aka Kaseem

Terence Jeffries

J.M. Benjamin
Author, Publisher, Motivational Speaker,

Dear Brothers,

I open this missive with the salutations *"Peace"*. And it is my sincere hope that you may find it while in your current state. I myself had to find peace some years ago as a means of survival and maintaining tool while dwelling in the "Belly of the Beast" known to us as prison. Though you don't know me personally, I'm positive our lives are in fact very similar. As you read this letter you'll realize that we have a lot in common. In hopes of making you comfortable as well as receptive to what it is I have to say in this notation allow me to properly introduce myself in order to bridge the gap between strangers.

My name is J.M. Benjamin and I am an author. I've contributed a short story titled *"Keepin' It Gangsta"* to an anthology titled 'Menace II Society', contributed another short story titled *"Charge It To the Game"* to an anthology titled "Street Chronicles" and I wrote the newly released hot street novel *'Down In The Dirty'*.

More personally, I am a Muslim man baring the attribute Mustafa which means the *"chosen one"*. I am also a father of three; two girls and one boy. But before I was the author, the Muslim man or the father, I was simply known as Squirm from the projects out in Plainfield New Jersey. The nickname Squirm was given to me by my mother when I was a baby because she said I used to squirm around a lot when I was little. In the 'hood, something as innocent as a nickname given to one by his mother can eventually become corrupted and come to represent negativity.

You see, I was once just like you, starting out in life innocently and then ultimately becoming a negative product of my environment. Over 12 years ago circumstances, recklessness, and bad choices lead me to where you find yourself today and where I have been since 1994, locked down. I've spent the better part of my 12 years incarcerated trying to repair the damage that I've done to myself and ease the pain that I've caused others, most of all my Mother.

I was just like you, spreading chaos and mayhem within my community and wherever else I traveled. But notice how I used the word *was,* because I can honestly say to you, I am a different man today then I was back then. I am not gonna pretend that it was an easy journey to reach where I am in life today because I would be lying to you, but nevertheless it was a journey worth taking. When I look back at the type of individual I was and look at the type of individual I am today, my transition has been especially rewarding .

Nothing in life comes easy and change is probably the hardest mission for anyone to partake in. But I've learned the best joys in life are the joys you have to work hard for. Which is why I sit here today ready to pour you a tall glass of my past, my present and my intended future in the hopes that I may put something positive on your mind and place some hope in your heart. At the same time I wish to open your eyes to the harsh realities and the grim consequences which result from the choices we make in the street life. This is my contribution to my brother

Moe Betta's quest to break the chains that keep bringing us back to prison over and over again. I'm living proof that you can put an end to the revolving door prison cycle and turn your negative into a positive.

Allow me however long it takes to bring you on my journey. A journey of where I come from, where I've been, where I am today and where I plan to go in the future. Give yourself the opportunity to free your mind from the prison walls and the prison mentality which keeps so many of us stagnate while we're incarcerated. It's my sincere hope, through this letter that I can inspire all those who've traveled the same roads I've once traveled to change their game plans. My brothers, there is no progression without struggle first.

"How dare you bring this junk into my house! I'll be dead in my grave if I let you disrespect me like this! I'll see you in jail first! You gonna be just like your father."

Those are the words that I've carried around with me for the past 20 years of the 32 years I have been in existence. They are the words my mother said to me the day she discovered the drugs I had brought into her house. Words that have haunted me since that day. The last thing I ever wanted to become in life was like my father. A lot of y'all can relate to that. But as I continued to indulge more and more into negativity, despite my mother's pleas and complaints, I had in fact become just like my father in so many ways.

For as far back as I can remember, the only memories I have of my father are of him running the streets and in and out of prison more than he was home. We don't realize how much of an effect not having a father around while we're young has on us until we are men and fathers ourselves. As I got older I had even managed to emulate my father's womanizing behavior and reckless ways of living; fathering 3 children of my own by different women. Now here it was, I had practically followed in my father's footsteps. My reckless lifestyle was now creating the same distant memories in my own children mind as he did in mine.

It wasn't until I was seven years old when I learned that I had a brother a year and a half older than me living right across the train tracks in another housing projects. My father wasn't even man enough at the time to admit that he had fathered another child outside of his marriage with my mother. Ironically, I met my brother through mutual acquaintances who noticed our stark resemblance. After the confirmation of our relation, the two of us became inseparable like Siamese twins.

There was only one time I can actually recall my father trying to step up to the plate to be the man me and my siblings needed him to be. By that time it was already too late because the damage had long ago been done.

I still remember it as if it were just yesterday and I am sure my father remembers it as well. It had been years since me or my brother had seen or heard from our father and he had just come home from Rahway state prison where he had practically lived. About this time me and my brother James (known as Peter Pan) had already been about three years deep in the drug game; me 14 years old, Pete 16. On this particular day I was in the hallway of building 524 in the 2nd St. housing projects in Plainfield indulging in an intense cee-low dice game, with me holding the bank. You know the drill; bets being placed, slick comments being made, everybody just hanging out having a good time. As I rolled the dice trying to roll an unbeatable point so I could fatten my bankroll, it suddenly got quieter than a thief in the night. You could see everyone's focused attention was drawn behind me. Instinctively my first thought was, whoever was behind me either had to be the police or the stickup kids with guns drawn. Either way it couldn't be a good look for me, so I thought. Slowly turning around I was surprised to see the person standing before me was no other than my own father. In spite of all the resentment and animosity that I had built up in me for all the years of abandonment and the pain he put my mother through, for some reason I was happy to see him. We gave each other manly hugs and exited the dice game.

He just shook his head and grinned the way I sometimes do in disbelief. Nothing could have prepared me for what he said he wanted to talk to me and my brother about in private. Neither me or Pete could have imagined what he'd say to us that day.

"Listen", he began, *"I have been hearing about you two dudes all throughout the system. A lot of people talking about how my two sons got it going on out here, how y'all out here running wild. I blame myself for not being here for you, but I'm here now and all this nonsense is about to come to an end."*

At first I thought my ears were deceiving me. Here it was, me and my brother were practically seasoned veterans in the game;

had been to the youth house, carried guns, purchased expensive cars, jewelry, partied and dwelt in places we weren't even old enough to be in. We were having sex with females way older then us, exposed to the best liquor money could buy and familiar with every profitable illegal drug in existence. On top of all that, we were indulging in a long list of other pleasures and vices that living the fast life consisted of. Now just like that, my father comes outta the clear blue sky and think he's gonna put a stop to what me and Pete would live and die for. At the time I would've respected him more if he had just asked us to give him enough money to get back on his feet or even to take him shopping.

Being the man I am today and as I reflect back on his words, I have to respect him for his attempt to reach out and save his sons from the streets. I couldn't understand that back then. He wanted to save us from the same lifestyle that basically destroyed his life.

As me and my brother stood there dumbfounded trying to figure out what possessed our pops to come at us like that, it was apparent my brother felt the same as me, only he voiced his feelings for the both of us. I still remember my brother saying what he said to our father as if he had just spoken the words prior to my writing this.

"Where were you when our mothers were struggling? Huh?" He questioned my father. *"Don't try to come home and try to be no father now, it's too late for that"*, he added and he had never lied.

My father was 14 years too late for me and 16 years too late for my brother to try and dictate what we could and couldn't do. He had lost that right and authority years ago and he knew it, which is why he had no comeback response to my brother's statement. Instead, he made an about face and exited our apartment. He retreated like someone who was fully aware that he'd lost, not only the battle but the war as well.

Now that I've grown up and matured in life, I often wondered what had transpired between me, my brother and our father that day in our apartment when he came to *save us*. What effects did that day have on him to the day we heard he was back in the streets hustling again. Ironically, months later me and my brother would actually found ourselves joining forces with our father as he took our knowledge of the game to new heights. He would be the one who'd introduce us to the drug game in the South, a move that would later change my life forever and not for the better.

My father would admit to me and my brother later on how the confrontation at our apartment had hurt him deeply in a way he never been hurt before.

It would take me until I reached manhood to understand the direct correlation between my father's absence in my life and his reckless lifestyle, to the choices I had been making and the lifestyle I had been living. I look for no excuses and offer no blame, but as most of us know now, growing up without a strong father in the home and in our life puts us at a disadvantage at an early age. No matter how much a mother loves her son or sons, no matter how much she tries to protect

195

them, it's not the same as having a father in a son's life. Without that much needed guidance a father is supposed to give his son, the son goes through young adulthood trying to find his way alone. Easily influenced by the negativity which surrounds him.

As a man and a father of three beautiful children I sometimes fear my own children having similar words for me, like my brother had for our father, upon my release from prison. My son was born while I was incarcerated and my daughters were only eight months and one year old when I went away. They are now turning 11, 12 and 13. They have not had me in their lives a full year yet. That's something shames me. It is partially because of that reason I decided to work on bettering myself while confined. Using them as motivational fuel for my vehicle of change.

Most of us are fathers now and we have to understand the damage that we do to our children by not being out there with them. Especially when it comes to our daughters. A father is the first man a daughter forms a bond with and without that bond a lot of times daughters go astray in many different ways then boys do. The decisions we make affect so many people. My father's lifestyle and reckless ways kept him from being a part of my life, my lifestyle and reckless ways have kept me from being a part of my children's life, but unlike my father when he was going back and forth to prison I have been using my incarceration as a growing experience. I didn't want to come home like my father did and have my children reject me, so I knew I had to make some drastic changes in my life.

Despite my father's shortcomings, my mother, like most of the single mothers struggling to raise their kids in the 'hood, was and still remains till this day a superwoman. As a single parent she tried to provide a good life for me and my siblings. My mother has always seen to it that we knew there was life beyond the ghetto. She instilled in all of us the morals, respect, and qualities that a parent does for a child. Unfortunately like many of us living and growing up in poverty stricken communities, we sometimes become creatures of our environment.

While my moms was out there busting her hump working multiple jobs, going to school, and trying to give us the best life possible I was being educated in the streets by those who dwelt in them.

There was no way my mother could be there to hold my hand 24 hours a day, seven days a week, and still be able to provide me with the basic necessities. I could never find her at fault or to blame for taking the wrong roads in life, as a kid she instilled in me the difference between right and wrong, I simply chose the latter.

For acceptance from my peers I made bad decisions, sometimes consciously. Because of that, I had to face and deal with the consequences and repercussions behind making those bad decisions. My mother used to always say, *"a hard head makes a soft behind."* It wasn't until I went to prison I realized the depth of her words.

By the time I was 16, me and my brother had climbed up the criminal ladder, making names for ourselves in the streets.

Names that were being mentioned in the same breath as some of those who we had idolized, admired and looked up to when we were younger. Our names were ringing bells now. You know how it goes when you become a neighborhood/street/ghetto celebrity.

One of the worst decisions I made was when I decided to quit school. An above average student, I was getting A's and B's when I dropped out in my 10th grade year to run the streets full-time. My brother quit in the ninth grade. When we were young a whole lot of us chose street smarts over book smarts. And as the saying goes, *"had I known what I know now, I would not have done some of the things that I did."* And that's real talk!

With the decision to abandon my education behind me, I traveled back and forth down south to get my hustle on by any means possible. Imagine two young dudes with no license barely able to see over the dashboard and steering wheel pushing these expensive whips. We were so out of control, we were going O.T. (out of town to hustle) in the kitted out whip, system booming and the whole nine. Ridin' dirty with a car full of drugs not even knowing or caring for that matter, that each trip we took we were traveling with a life sentence in the trunk. To us it was simply a way of life. You can get so caught up in the streets that you begin to see nothing wrong with the things you're doing until the day comes when reality slaps the taste outta ya mouth. That day came for me just like it came for you, when the fun turned serious and the consequences real.

Me and my brother were in the South just as much as we were in New Jersey. We was traveling up and down I95 frequently. Usually we took turns making the trip back and forth down south and this particular trip was his turn. For nothing more than my own selfish reasons I convinced him to let me go back to Jersey for the re-up instead. Honestly speaking, I was only eager to get home to see my then girlfriend and show everyone that Pete and Squirm were *'doing their thing out of state'*. Something a lot of dudes, even older dudes from around our way didn't have heart enough to do back then. We're talking about 1988-1989.

Against his better judgment my brother Pete agreed to let me go this trip. As if he were psychic or probably just knowing me, I remember him saying, *"yo go straight up and take care of business, then jump on the last bus back down."* That was the plan, but you know in the game nothing goes the way you plan especially at age 16.

When I reached Jersey I mixed business with pleasure and that would have grave consequences. I took a detour from the initial agenda and because of that I found myself in the midst of a routine bus search when I finally did get back on track and heading back down south. Unbeknownst to me at the time, I had fit the ideal description to the police who were posted up at the bus terminal. A young African-American male traveling alone on a one-way ticket from New York. This misfortune cost me nearly 2 years out of my life in an adult prison at age 16. It also cost me to lose the girlfriend I was dealing with and the child she was carrying at the time when she decided to have an abortion. You would think that my losses would've been enough to make me change my life... That was far from the case.

The only good thing that came out of this situation was my finishing school. I received my GED while locked down.

During this short period of incarceration I did what I had to do to project an appearance of change. But the truth of the matter is I was counting down the days until Squirm was able to get back on the block and back to business. Besides, my brother was still out there representing for the both of us. I wasn't ready to change, nor did I feel there was a need to. If I had somehow managed to see the wisdom in changing, my brother had made it hard for me to do so anyway. I walked right back into the street life the first day I was released. During my 2 year stint my brother made sure I needed for nothing. He took care of me while I was away and when I came home he made sure I wanted for nothing. He provided me with all the hustler accessories; a car, money, jewelry and the crew he put together. Within a week's time I was back knee deep in the game. I got my hustle swagger back and it was as if I had never spent one day in prison.

There's a saying that goes, *"if you fail to plan then you plan to fail."* And that's the best way to describe what took place with me. I had basically failed the first day I was released from prison, like so many brothers do, because the only plan I had was really no plan at all. My returning to prison was inevitable.

In the short period of time I was on the streets, I managed to father three children, catch numerous cases and become a fugitive of justice. My life was in shambles and the streets began to take its toll on me. I put myself in life-threatening situations on numerous occasions and caused my love ones to lose plenty of sleep over the life I was living. My mother would always fret about getting that dreadful phone call or late night knock on the door, telling her I was found dead somewhere.

When I was finally apprehended my reckless lifestyle finally caught up to me. I received a lengthy prison sentence by the state and a lengthy federal prison sentence to drive the point home I guess. When it was all said and done, in total, I would have to give the system 13 years of my 32 years of living.

Over 10 years ago I embraced Islam, but it wasn't until I submitted wholeheartedly that I began to find peace of mind. State prison being what it is, it was a constant struggle for me to maintain that peace of mind. Nevertheless, I had worked on changing for the six years I was in the state, but deep down inside I knew I hadn't changed enough. When I entered the federal prison system, the reality of the further changes I needed to make began to set in.

When I was in the state system I was only allowed to have visitation with loved ones from behind a plexiglass partition because of my involvement with selling drugs in prison.

My first family visit in Federal prison, minus any partitions, came when my mother flew in from Indianapolis to see me for my birthday. Prior to this visit, my mother had visited me in prison before but now that there was no plexigl partition to separate us this visit was the most emotional visit the two of us had ever had.

I'll never forget the look in my mother's eyes. For a minute she just stared at me and I remember asking her what was wrong. *"I cannot do this anymore Squirm this is it"*, she said as tears began to spill out her eyes, painting her face as they cascaded down her cheeks. In this very emotional moment I realized just how much pain I was causing my mother; the very woman who brought me into this world. I felt ashamed. Ashamed I had hurt my mother in some of the same ways my father had hurt her. It was hard for me to reach out and console my mother knowing that I too had become the source of her pain.

Because of the guilt I felt, it was hard for me to reach out to my mother for the first few months when I was transferred to federal prison. In many ways the plexiglass partition that separated us in the state visitation room served as a buffer zone between me, her, and the pain I caused her. Now seeing my mother with nothing standing between us was painful. My reckless lifestyle, rash decisions and lust for the street way of life had caused my mother so much pain and I didn't know how to tell her how truly sorry I was.

My mother had always been there for me unconditionally and had it not been for a letter she had written me, I don't think I would've known how to reach out to her while I remained in prison. As I sat in my room and began to read the letter my mother had written, the opening lines stood out to me as if I was reading them with 3-D glasses on. Lines that actually brought uncontrollable tears to my eyes. Lines that opened the spigot of tears to the point of almost making the letter unreadable. These were the words that had broken me down like a double barreled shotgun.

"Dear son, I want to know that no matter what, I will always be proud to have you as my child and I will always love you."

No matter how far I had fallen in life my mother has always been there to pick me up. When I forgot who I was and what I was capable of, she was always there to remind me that I could do big things. I had taken my mother through so much and with her soothing words she was able to ease the guilt that I had been carrying with me all these years, in a way only a mother could do.

It was during this period of my life I was in the process of making major transitions for the better. You see, everyone has a limitation in life and I believe I had finally reached mine. I began to really evaluate my life. I started by weighing the pros and the cons of my choices, my actions and my thinking. And at the end of my tally I came to the conclusion that, in spite of what I thought was living the good life when I was hustlin' in the streets, when it was all said and done none of it had been worth it. The materialistic creature comforts that I had accumulated and enjoyed for a short period of time wasn't worth sacrificing my freedom, nor the relationship with my mother and all the other people who cared for me.

I knew then that I needed a change from within and the only way I could do that was, by making the decision to do so. I sought guidance in my belief and began to participate in some of the programs available to me inside the institution. It was in one of those programs that a teacher helped me discover my love and craft in writing. This teacher had advised me to keep a journal and use it as an outlet whenever I felt stressed, discouraged or even encouraged.

Initially, I wasn't feeling this but out of respect for her I calmly accepted the notebook and promised to utilize it. Prison life being what it is, even after all of the self- reconstruction I had been doing, I still managed to return to solitary confinement for a frivolous confrontation that turned into something physical. A few days later the teacher had come to see me in lockup. I was somewhat embarrassed to tell her what had happened knowing how she had held me in such high regard. She treated me not as an inmate but as a human being.

After I explained what happened I still remember what she said in response, *"sometimes things happen and we can't let them get in the way of what we have to do in life. Why don't you take your journal and use it to write about your life and maybe you'll figure out where you keep going wrong."*

Who would've thought those words would have such a major impact on my life and play such a decisive role in securing my future. As suggested, I began to utilize the journal book. Beginning with my earliest recollections as a child of a dysfunctional family I examined the behavior of my parents, particularly my father.

Ultimately, what started out as a therapeutic phase for me blossomed into a 400 plus page manuscript about my life. And even though this was not the material that would eventually land me a two book publishing contract it was the material that motivated me to continue my writing and strive for a career in the literary field. Since discovering what I believe to be one of my many hidden talents, writing had become the basis of my life and a form of discipline for me. Rather than participate in some of the unhealthy or stagnant activities one will find in prison I chose to commit myself to perfecting my craft. The way I see it, when I was out in the streets hustlin' I had dedicated all of my time and energy into doing that. I figured the same energy I had used then for something negative could be channeled into something positive now.

An old head had told me once that, *"there is a difference between a drug dealer and a hustler."* He'd say, *"they are not one of the same."* The old head explained it like this, *"the drug dealer can only sell drugs. The hustler can sell anything." Since I've been writing I have proven to myself and to those who matter to me most that I am not a mere drug dealer, but a natural born Hustler. I have grown in all aspects, not only as a writer, but as a man, a father and son, brother and friend.*

I'd like to say to you, that for me, prison was a necessary journey and stepping stone in order for me to get my life back on the right track. In closing I would also like to add that, prison is what you make of it. Regardless to its conditions and what you're subjected to, Allah has instilled in us all 'free will' and you have a choice to make the necessary changes in your life. So it is up to you to make the best out of what you feel or believe to be the worse. You can't go wrong by CHANGIN' YOUR GAME PLAN!!

First and foremost as always, I want to thank The Most High, for granting me the strength and knowledge to share a glimpse of my journey and transition with you all. He is truly the greatest. To my friend and comrade Mr. Randy Kearse thanks for the opportunity to be apart of this positive and powerful project. Just a year ago we walked the federal prison track passing mere thoughts back and forth. Today our thoughts have become our reality. To my family and a few selective friends, all of your love, support, and encouragement in the past as well as the present has not gone unnoticed. I am grateful to have you all in my corner, thanks for everything. Most importantly, to the brothers and sisters currently behind the wall, let my contribution and testimony be an inspiration for change. I wish you all freedom and success!

J.M.Benjamin www.allaboutjmbenjamin.com

J.M.Benjamin is the author of two of the street's best selling novels **Down In The Dirty** *and* **My Manz an'nim** *and* **Ride or Die Chicks.** *A contributing author to the anthology* **Menace II Society.** *Look for a short story by J.M. in an upcoming anthology published by Urban Anthologies titled* **That Dude**. *He is also CEO of Real Edutainment Publishing Inc.*

Storm Weeks Aka **Kaseem,**
Author, *Pit Fighter*

I am a 40 year old black male who has spent 22 of the last 23 years in a prison cell. Do the math and that means that more than half my life has been spent behind bars. By the time I finish this present prison sentence I will have been locked up a little over 28 years. And the sad thing about it is that I have no one else to blame but myself.

Sure, I can attribute my incarceration to the inequalities that exist in this country. I could say that racism and the monetary gain produced by the prison expansion industry played an important part too. The product of my environment could also be used to explain my confinement. I can suggest that all of the above factors had a hand in me landing in prison but I won't. Ultimately, I am to blame for my lack of freedom.

Anger was my downfall. Couple that anger with a bunch of bad choices and I am a prime candidate for this prison ID number. Consider this piece of information a case study on how not to go to prison because of the mistakes that I've made. Discard this information and you may one day suffer my same fate.

To understand a man you must first know the child. I was a angry child from the start. That anger came from growing up in an extremely dysfunctional family. Seeing and going through things that no child should ever experience made me very jaded toward life as I became older. The rage I felt festered and boiled over when I came of age in the city streets. I never started trouble, but I sure knew how to end it. Any ghetto in any part of the world is the breeding grounds for unbound violence. In order not to succumb to the violence I had to partake in it. At first I got my scrawny butt kicked a whole lot of times, but I was a fast learner and I started to kick a whole lot of butt myself. I'm a staunch supporter of an eye for an eye and do unto others before they do unto you. I have blackened many eyes and did on to many others before they did me. Since I was small for my age and light in the butt to boot, I had to prove myself over and over again before people got the hint. Sometimes I would have to fight two and three times a day. Soon that bygone era of fighting with the hands played out and people traded in their knuckle-game for knives and guns. I went right along with that trend. It wasn't long afterward that my quest to spill blood landed me in a prison cell.

At the age of 17 I was arrested for murder. Although I was only 5'8" and 130 pounds, I had a chip on my shoulder the size of Mount Everest. The transition from the harsh streets to the harsher reality of prison life wasn't hard for me because of my anger. If the streets allowed me to get some anger and frustration off, the prison system let me vent my rage to the fullest of my abilities.

The adolescent detention center I was first placed in housed pretrial prisoners between the ages of 16 to 21. It was a pure gladiator school. Putting young men together with a whole lot of time on their hands and nothing constructive on their mind created a very volatile environment. The young prisoners had to be separated from the older ones because of the problems that came about from putting the two groups in the same facility. Although the younger criminals were doing time, kids will be kids and they involved themselves in a heap of trivial bullsiht. Most of the time the violence was sparked from the littlest of things. Just bumping into or stepping on someone's foot could get a person stabbed or slashed in the face with a razor. Other discrepancies arose from the use of the telephone, the taking of jewelry or any other personal items that a prisoner might have. All in all, it was a dog-eat-dog world and only the strongest survived.

Once I was sentenced for my crimes I went to an upstate prison. It was there that the adolescent criminals were integrated with the older ones. Of course there were problems between the age groups due to the generational gap, but those differences didn't affect me since I stayed out of the way and minded my own business. If anything did come my way I held my own and dealt with it accordingly.

I was young, wild and with no sense of direction. Although I was not a troublemaker, trouble had a way of finding me. Because of that trouble I made the circuit of some of the various prisons around the state. I bounced around a lot and didn't stay in one place too long. On one of my journeys through the criminal justice system I happened upon a particular prison that would eventually change my life.

It was there that I met a good-hearted individual. This prisoner worked in the school building as a tutor, he had been locked up awhile and was about to go home in a year or two. He saw an essay I wrote for one of the school's entrance exams and took a interest in me. This individual told me that I was far from stupid and that if I kept on the path that I was on I would eventually kill someone or would get myself killed and shipped home in a wooden box. He also made a strong point, by often saying, *"spending the rest of your life in a stinking prison was for suckers"*, he would so patiently explain to me. It was then that he tried to get me to sign up for the college programs (this was at a time when TAP and PELT grants were still available to prisoners). I wasn't trying to hear any of that advice and only agreed to sign up for college courses so that he'd leave me alone. Weeks later he brought the textbooks to me, he said he knew that I wasn't coming to the books so he brought the books to me. Reluctantly I entered the program.

Months later I saw this same prisoner murdered right before my very eyes. He was killed because he was trying to squash a beef between two other prisoners. He only had a couple of months left on his sentence. The administration sent him home in a wooden box. That one incident changed my whole perspective. I calmed down and started taking life more seriously. Education became my primary concern and it helped keep me sane in the midst of the madness that goes on in prison.

After five years and eight months I was released from prison. I was almost 22 years old and happy to be getting out of hell alive. Once I was on the streets a couple months I decided to continue the educational route because I only needed a few more credits for my associates degree.

Life was good, for so I thought. Ten months after being released from prison I was arrested for an attempted murder charge that I had absolutely nothing to do with. It was a bogus charge trumped up by the police because they needed someone to blame it on. I was the usual suspect and found myself back in the living hell that was prison.

I flipped out. There was no way on earth I could comprehend being locked up again, especially for something I didn't do. The first few weeks I thought the case of mistaken identity would be thrown out and I would go home. But that was not to be. The weeks turned into months and the months turned into a year and a half. Once more I was subjected to a cage way of life. All of my pent-up anger came roaring back out again. I took on a *'me against the world'* attitude and gave up all hope of ever seeing the streets again. The pressure started to get to me. My first son was born during that time and I wasn't there to witness his birth. My girlfriend was beefing hard because I came back to jail. Family members turned their backs on me because they thought I didn't learn my lesson from the first prison stint.

Being in the overcrowded, stinking and violent fueled prison for the second go-around made me feel as if no matter what I did I was destined to be locked out for the remainder of my life. Faced with a life sentence for something I never did, I became even more angry and saw no way out of my predicament.

Seventeen months later I was vomited back out into society without even as much as an apology by the court system or the police for their mistake. During the whole time my life was in limbo, the victim of the crime I was supposedly to have committed, never came back to court to identify me as the perpetrator. After all that time I was finally given a bail.

I made bail and went on a rampage. As soon as I was released I hit the streets with a vengeance. In my mind I felt that somehow the world owed me and I was going to make someone pay for the pain and suffering. School wasn't even an option anymore. How could it be? I tried that straight and narrow path before and all it did was get me nowhere except for back to a prison cell again. This time around I didn't care about anything except for trying to make up for the lost time was stolen from me. That irrational thinking almost cost me my life. I lasted almost 3 months on the streets before the Feds locked me up.

My brief reign of terror in the free world ultimately earned me a 24 1/2 year sentence in federal prison.

Out of about 24 years I have to do 21 years and change. As of this writing I have 15 years in for the sentence with six more years to go. Was it worth it? Hell no! I am rotting away in some prison because I let my anger get the best of me. That anger clouded my mind and impaired my better judgment. I cannot point the finger at no one but myself. I was my own worst enemy.

The moral of this story is that, if anger is left unchecked it may very well destroy you. Myself and countless others just like me are shining examples of that fact. America has over 2 million people in prison and it leads the world and locking up its citizens.

If you do not want to become one of those statistics then you better not go down the road that I have traveled. Take it from me that road is long, hard and very cold.

Channel that fury toward something positive instead of taking that negative journey that would lead you straight to a hell made of concrete walls, razor wire, metal bars and lost souls. Learn to cage that fury within yourself before someone cages you and your fury for the rest of your life.

I've let go of the bitterness and anger that caused my situation. During my incarceration I've learned how to be humble and be appreciative of life. Through my writing I've found peace of mind. I look forward to the future and the challenges that accompany it. Though my journey has been long I can say that it hasn't been a wasted one. I know if I can look toward the future with hope and enthusiasm so can you.

Terence Jeffries, CEO

City Of Refuge Ministries and Outreach Program
TRUE FREEDOM

"Stolen water is sweet; food eaten in secret is delicious! What little do they know that the dead are there, that her guests are in the deaths of the grave." Proverbs 9:17, 18

I remember very early on in my incarceration, while at Fort Dix Federal correctional institution, better known as "The Dix", sitting in the TV room watching a movie and just doing time. Unbeknownst to me that the author of this book, Randy Kearse (Moe Betta) was hidden amongst the 50 or so inmates gathered in the TV room to watch the weekly institutional movie as well. As the movie ended and the credits started to roll, the complaints from the "Siskel and Eberts" of the bunch of inmates who had been watching the movie also began to roll. *"That was some straight trash". "Man, that was a waste of my time". "I know President Bush could do better than that!"* Heading for the stairs Moe and I could still hear the murmuring among the dudes and then, almost simultaneously, we went on to voice our opinions to one to another. Strange how two people could be of the same mind. We both had captured what we considered to be the brightest spot of the movie. The spot took only seven seconds and consisted of 16 words, but for us it made the whole movie worth watching.

"You get two lives to live... one you learn with and one you live with after."

These words I don't say served as the motivating force behind either Moe's or my own transformation while incarcerated but what I will say is, there is so much truth to those words. In those words we make our reality and encourage others to make theirs as well. I believe we have discovered the highest degree that life offers; without losing our lives. With that experience we can go forth in life with insight which cannot be bought and foresight that is preternatural. Most of all inspire someone to use their own life experiences to go forward in the future.

My contribution to this book will be in the area of spiritual transformation, the road that God's grace has brought me down. Except for the early part of my incarceration, my journey has been a walk with Jesus. I plan to be as transparent as possible without turning anyone off as I take you down my stony road traveled. Beginning to end leaving all the glory to those who have something to glory about, my main objective here is to point you to Jesus! "To him who is able to do unmeasurable more than all we can ask or imagine." The one who can wipe away your past, give you strength for today and hope for tomorrow. That you to may consider, CHANGAN' YOUR GAME PLAN!

When I was a child I spoke as a child, I understood as a child, I thought as that child..." CORINTHIANS 13:11a

Often times we associate the word child with a young male or female or attribute it to even a unborn baby. In my case I found it to be the definition at the bottom of Webster's list of definitions for the word child (child; childish person). It was my state of mind and it had nothing to do with my being young or old. As I look back on my sorry life I can truly say that immaturity was the disease I was plagued with for the first 33 years of my life (just seven short years ago). I was a child trapped in a man's body. Now after having seven long years to look back over my life and examine it with a new heart, eyes and ears; this one thing I can say, *"I once was lost but now I'm found, was blind but now I see"* John 9:25

In 1984, after being too stubborn and hardheaded for the Marine Corps I was shipped back to "da hood" from the bright and sunny climate of Paris Island South Carolina to the doom and gloom of the worse part of Brooklyn, New York; Brownsville a.k.a. *the ville.* Just in time to jump aboard the "crack express". I call it the "crack express" because this locomotive makes only two stops; the prison yard or the grave yard. All of the points in between you must jump off on your own if you are man enough to do so against great pressures. Actually, at this point in my life, I had never seen any drugs except on TV. Sports had filled the first 18 years of my life along with honest and honorable hustling (newspaper route, snow shoveling, packing and carrying groceries).

Upon my return to the 'hood I immediately got a job and started attending John J. College of criminal justice in Manhattan. This got old fast; so in 1986 I went off to attend Shaw University in Raleigh, North Carolina. Little did I know this was the beginning of my end, the unofficial start of my downfall. Instead of a college education my parents thought I was receiving, I would begin my studies in "Street Economics" and receive hands-on experience when it came to the power of supply and demand. Up until this point I was simply known as *Shake the Athlete* by my family and friends but because Satan had huge plans for me, once I got into the mix of things I would drop the athlete part and go by Shake. The name as well as the person now known as just Shake would do what had to be done to represent this alter image.

Raleigh NC or the "Research Triangle Area" as it is also known was filled with colleges and the college lifestyle was in full swing when I arrived at Shaw. But Raleigh was secretly becoming the jewel of the south for drug dealers. Washington DC and Virginia were becoming too hot and violent for New Yorkers on their O.T. (out of town) mission and North Carolina provided the perfect ground for migration. As fate (what I now know to be providence) would have it, I would become one of the original pioneers who'd open the flood gates of drugs moving in and cash flowing out of Raleigh (along with names of dudes that are dead, doing long prison sentences and who are still on the run to this day.) I dare not mention names but pray that God would show them the same grace and mercy that he has shown me. But I can mention Raleigh is where I did meet Randy Kearse A.k.a. Moe Betta and his brothers almost 20 years ago. Three grimy get money brothers with hearts of stone and the gun-game to back them.

Raleigh quickly became the drug jewel of the South. Some fought, some shot, and some even killed in an attempt to get every dollar Raleigh had. Money and egos got the best of all of us and we all had plenty of both. What's truly remarkable is during it all Moe, his brothers, and I didn't kill one another.

Which would've seem a more likely scenario then us writing a book together today.

"before his downfall a man's heart is proud..." Proverbs 18:12

The combination of street smarts and education proved to be my ruin. In my eyes there was no one smarter than "I", wiser than "I" and definitely not more craftier than "I". Like Satan, I had attempted to exalt myself above God. My goal was to be a ghetto superstar, a respected player in the so-called *game* and a known kingpin in the underworld. To accomplish that I was putting work on every block in every city I could. Sex, drugs and Hip-Hop was my diet and I began to create a monster that only fast money, fast cars and fast women could satisfy and only death or a long prison sentence could stop.

At the beginning of this ride is where I met my sweetheart Vanessa. She had transferred to Shaw University from Chaney State in Pennsylvania along with her sister. When I look back, if it weren't for our beautiful daughter Whitney I would give a arm to have had Vanessa and her sister choose another school so there would be a chance we would've never met. The street / hustlin' roller coaster ride I took her on for the next twelve years after we met and then the abandonment she's had to feel for the last seven years has left her deeply wounded. Doubts and regrets have caused even her to consider what her life might have been if we had never met.

When you live this kind of lifestyle you think you've gained so much while you're out there caught up in your "hustler's moment", but you lose things that no amount of money can get back. I sold not only my soul, but I sold out the very people who truly believed in me. The relationships and the friendships that were ruined, damaged and even destroyed by the choices I made back then is something I never took the time consider.

"Whatever a man sows, that he will reap. For he who sews to his flesh, will of the flesh reap corruption." GALATIANS 6:8a

On September 13, 1999 the U.S. Marshals tracked me down to an apartment I was renting outside of the Atlanta GA area. I had just moved there only months before from another location in that area trying to stay two steps ahead of *'the game'*. The trail had heated up because of several outstanding warrants and the countless times I bailed out and then jumped bail. But a little over a year before; I had successfully bonded out on the Feds under an alias and with an already outstanding Federal warrant against me on top of that. That particular incident had caused to serve the Feds some serious embarrassment, which just made them all the more eager and determined to apprehend me.

About 2:00pm in the afternoon, that dreadful Monday, I was supposedly opening the door for the meddling maintenance man, but to my surprise there were three armed white men introducing me the floor and a cold pair of handcuffs. My only response was the pathetic one you see on Cops each week given by the guilty. It's the humble and properly spoken *"What is it Sir?" "What have I done?"* response given by the guiltiest of suspects. A response given and dressed with respect, in hopes that it will throw the police and make them think they have the wrong person. We know it never works, not on TV and definitely not in real life. Ignoring my humble pleas for some answers they proceeded to search the apartment. A few minutes passed by and they told me their reason for the raid. They said, *"that 'The North side Rapist' was seen running in my apartment."* (This was a serial rapist who was terrorizing Atlanta at the time). They then went on to ask, *"what is your name?"* Whenever there is question there's hope – they must not have all the facts! I gave them my alias; they asked for identification. I said to myself, *"they really don't know how I am."* More hope! *"I have a chance." "I can bluff my way outta this",* my mind is telling me. I directed them to my driver's license, birth certificate and W2 forms all recently purchased in the alias name and they were convinced (at least that's what I thought). They apologized, (playing me to the fullest*), "Sorry Sir for the inconvenience, you're not the man we're looking for."* A slight pause.. long enough for me to say, *"Thank God."* (and turn my arms slightly for them to take the handcuffs). *"Then maybe you can help us?"* one of them said. *"We're looking for a black male about your size, about your age 33 years old, from Brooklyn, NY, named Terence Jeffries A.k.a. Shake, A.k.a. Xavier, A.k.a. Sha, A.k.a. Malek- could you help us?"* With that I just sunk my head in the carpet and within *"my life is over."*

Thoughts of Vanessa, Tyshan, Whitney and my Moms, all that meant something to me began to flash through my mind. They were about to be stripped from me and life as I knew it was about to be changed. What hurt the most was that there was nothing I could do about it. Satan had won, he had succeeded in his plan to destroy me; or did he?

"Vanity of Vanities" Says the Preacher; "Vanities of Vanities, all is Vanity." Ecclesiastes 1:2

After my arrest and subsequent extradition, I found myself at the Pitt County Detention Center in Greenville, NC facing a lengthy prison sentence of ten years to life imprisonment. I was charged with conspiracy, counterfeiting, obstruction of justice among a host of other charges. With the prospect of doing all that time and being stripped from love ones; I can honestly say behind bars nothing about me had changed. I will admit to having many sleepless nights over my fate, but for the most part, nothing about me had changed. I will also admit to some casual reading of scripture and praying here and there, but for the most part, nothing about me had changed. I was still fiendin' for the rush of making a fast dollar. Unable to deal in real currency, in jail we substitute rubber band stacks of green for anything of value; personal property, food items, stamps and/or cigarettes.

Upon my arrival to the county jail I immediately went to work establishing a black-market prison store where I loaned one food item for two in return. From there it was cuffing the Monopoly dice and starting my own little dice game. From the dice game I branched out into running a poker game and not long after that I went to bankrolling a sports gambling ticket. By the time I was in full swing, the cell block I was being housed in was nicknamed, Lil Vegas and every inmate in the building wanting to be transferred where the action was. After adding on the big hands to insure collections and payments, I was on easy street. With all that was facing me I still continued to roll. I know a lot of us laughed to keep from crying, but for the most, nothing about me had changed.

There was only one hitch in the operation, every night about 7pm I had to shut Lil Vegas down. Out of respect, guys would abandon the gambling activities to listen to the Christian volunteers who would come to the jail to minister to anyone who would listen. A lot of the southern men were raised in the church, around church folks and had respect for the Christian volunteers. Not me! They were in the way of me getting my 'hustle' on. In order to keep my frustration from showing, when the Christian volunteers showed up I'd pull some of the guys in to a cell with me to tell some of our *war stories* from the streets. To me, this was more interesting then listening to what the volunteers had to say. As the weeks went by we even added homemade wine to "our" nightly gathering. We'd brew jail "Alize" made from honey buns, kool aid, orange juice and jolly ranchers – strained through a doo-rag and it was lights out.

With everything we had lost and everything we were about to lose, we still tried our best to hold on to the streets. I think Puffy Daddy said it best, *"I thought I told y'all that we won't stop."* Yeah we were locked up, facing madd years, away from our families and we was still singing the same old song, *"thought I told you that we won't stop, I thought I told y'all that we won't stop! Uh un!"*

"...Woe to him who is alone when he falls, for he has no one to help him up." Ecclesiastes 4:10b

I remember one day getting off the phone from talking to my daughter and feeling very down. My daughter still had no idea where I was and all she knew was she wanted her daddy. She had been yelling on the phone *"it's not fair, it's not fair." "I want my father! When are you coming home!?"* I went dead silent on the phone. I had no answer to give her. It was at that moment that I started thinking the future looked hopeless and I had better start dealing with it. I went straight from the phone to a bible study some guys on the block had been holding nightly on the cell block. They were just about to close when I arrived, with smiles and opened arms they welcomed me in.

"Brother Jeffries we were just about to close out with prayer, please join us." The group formed a circle with clutched hands, *"Do you have any prayer requests?"* I was asked. (Gasp for breath! Stutter!) "Thank you for allowing me *'in'*", I said as my eyes began to tear up. My heart was heavy and after getting off the phone with my daughter, it felt like my heart was as a boulder. All these years of running the streets and being a thug, I could have stood there in the prayer circle and bawled like a baby. Sensing my vulnerability one of the brothers took over the prayer for me and simply said, *"Let us pray that God touches brother Jeffries heart and joins us more often in the future.*

For a little while it was business as usual, things pretty much ran as they always did, but, I began to sit in on the services when the volunteers came through (we'd hold deal until they left). Then one night the grace of God appeared, that grace that touches and teaches your heart to believe. That grace that says, "excuse me, may I have your bags", and boy was I carrying a load. The preacher who came that evening preached the word of God to my heart this night. And before he left he asked, "is there anyone who wants to give their life to Jesus this night?" With a little hesitation I came forward – the irresistible grace of the spirits calling at work. That's the night I laid all my burdens down. The man of God explained to me I was a new creature in Christ and that I was also Christ's ambassador. For some time there was little evidence or signs of change. The gambling continued, the store was still open and I kept the books tight and nothing that I was doing hinted that I was going to depart with any of these things.

Then one day God sent deliverance my way in a brother named Allie Aldridge. He was an elderly man about 6'1" with long hair and tattoos everywhere, he was a cross between Woodstock and the Ayrian Brotherhood. We were cell-mates for three days and in that time he displayed faith that I have yet to see in my seven years of incarceration. One night while we were talking, I shared with him that I did not want to continue doing the things that I was doing and live the way I had been living, yet professing to be a child of God. He said, *"you mean that?!"*, I said, *"Yes!"*, He said, *"Tell God, Jesus will take it way if you truly mean it."* That night I prayed to God as earnestly as my heart knew how and asked the Lord to take away everything and anything that was not like him. That he would do a work in me that would allow me to properly represent him. Jesus was true to his word he said, *"I tell you the truth, my father will give you whatever you ask in my name."* John 14:23

A hatred for all those things that I so much loved about the streets and the street mentality became my consuming passion. I started by giving away the prison store I had. Next I gave away the girlie magazines, I quit all gambling activities, all these things were now a thing of the past. The guys thought I was going crazy. I joined the bible study and soon started leading it. We started pre-lock-down prayer and I started to see my life changing. The grace of God (His unmerciful favor) that I had only read and heard about, I started to see manifest in my life. The more I began to read the word of God and meditate on it, the more God began to reveal Himself to me. Octavius Winslow in his masterpiece "The Work of the Holy Spirit" wrote precisely about the Spirits work in my life. He wrote:

"...in most cases... is a more gradual work. It is a work of time. The soul is placed in the school of deep experience and is led on step by step, stage by stage."

So true are these words they should be cannon!

"But when I became a man I put away childish things."

Corinthian 13:11b

God became a mirror before me; in whom I was able to see myself. The more and more He revealed Himself, the more and more I sighed, *"Oh wretched man that I am! Who will deliver me from this body of death? I thank God – through Jesus Christ our Lord!"* Romans 7:24, 25 God allowed me to see how bad off a condition I was still in! He showed me just what was in my heart and most of all, just how bad I was in need of a savior. Jesus Christ entered this world to rescue sinners of who I am the worst of them all.

My heart had deceived me for some 33 years. It led me to believe I was this misunderstood family man who had an exclusive plan of action for achieving life's goals. And that the end would justify the means. But the bible clearly states: *"There is a way that seems right to man, but in the end it leads to death."* Proverbs 16:28

Soon the transformation began to be seen by all. It was like discovering the ultimate club where you feel like you had the best time of your life, like you partied like you never partied in your life. The next morning you get on the phone and tell everybody and anybody about the hot new club you found and how you want them to come next week. You told them because you wanted them to share in your experience too. So to, I wanted everyone to know about Christ and share with me the experience of our Lord and Savior.

This transformation followed me on into the system once I was finally given my prison sentence with the Feds. I can remember my first time attending church as a Christian at FCI Petersburg in Petersburg, VA. From the beginning to the end, for one whole hour I cried and cried, all the while saying, *"I'm home, I'm home; this is where I belong"*, for one whole hour. That joy traveled with me all over that prison compound for the next few months until I was transferred to FCI Fort Dix, in Fort Dix NJ. Upon my arrival there I joined the church and became a regular member; attending both Sunday services and bible studies. But as I became more familiar with the institution, the more and more faces began to look familiar to me. Old friends and acquaintances who only wanted to remind me of who *"we was"*, *"what we did"* and how much fun *"it was"*.

One day while the CO was handing out mail at mail call, he called out a name that was oh to familiar to me. *"Randy Kearse!"* A voice from the back of the crowd said, *"pass it back!"* Though this name was very familiar to me the gentleman recovering the letter didn't fit the physical description, demeanor or character of the person I was connecting the name to. I had to check it out because I had a long and at times troubling friendship with his younger brother who hinted that I was behind him being shot several times over a money dispute (which to this day I honestly had nothing to do with that). And I also had an resolved beef with his older brother which ended in front of the Apollo Theater with our guns drawn and promises to see each other later. So it was in my best interest to approach him and extend my hand if he was the *"Randy Kearse"* I knew. The outcome I wasn't sure about but the importance I did know if I was really about change.

To my surprise when I approached him he expressed the same attitude towards the past as I held, he said, *"Look man, the past is the past. I'm trying to move on with my life. The past has no room in my future."* He went on to say, *"If there is anything I can do for you just let me know."* And a friendship started and grew from there, more obstacles moved out of our way. So many times people let what happened in the past stop them moving towards the future. We knew of each others past but we never sat around glorifying our misdeeds when we would talk, we talked about the promises and the challenges that future held for us. We talked about change and though he wasn't transformed through the spiritual he definitely recognized his blessings. Nonetheless he had found a place of peace after all his trials and tribulations.

Over the next few years God would stand by me when the tests came, prison being what it is, but I held my faith and each test made me stronger and stronger. As time passed, I was no longer known as "Shake" by those who knew me, instead it was Bro. Shake and Bro. Jeffries by those I recently met. God would use me mightily in that place as a vessel of honor and respect. Comforting others, bringing enemies together, giving the young men someone to look to other than the hype and lies seen in the music videos.

"We also glory in tribulations, knowing that tribulations produce perseverance; and perseverance, character; and character, hope." Romans 5:3-4

Even in such circumstances hope was restored. True hope, the only kind of hope that doesn't disappoint. I came to understand that life has purpose – not excluding my own. I let go and let God; refusing to allow Satan to corrupt my heart and thought. By believing God that *"all things work together for the good to those who love God."* Romans 8:28 Moreover I learned that true peace is experienced as grace is received. And that hope is actualized, when and only when, in our trials tribulations we allow our will to be swallowed up entirely in God's will.

When I came to prison seven years ago it seemed all hope was lost. I told my girl Vanessa, *"go on with your life, there's no hope for me."* I told my mother I was sorry for destroying my life and ending up useless. All hope at life, let alone a new life was gone. My surroundings said, *"you'll be 41 years old when you get out. No experience, a criminal record; what are you gonna do?"* Then I would remember old sayings like, *"you can't teach an old dog new tricks"* and *"Jail only makes smarter criminals."* But thanks be to God, when the bible says, *"He that has an ear, let him hear what the spirit says..."* I heard Him! When the bible says, *"For God so loved the world that He gave his only begotten Son, that whoever believes in* Him should not perish but have everlasting life." I believed Him! When the bible says, "Trust in the Lord with all your heart and lean not to your own understanding; In all your ways acknowledge Him, And he will direct your paths." I trusted Him!

Now I tell you, all who read this book – God, Changes your game plan! The same thing Jesus did for me, He will do for you, just let Him into your life. Had anyone had told me seven and a half years ago that I would be walking with Jesus today, I would thought they were crazy, but now that I'm walking with my Lord and Savior I was crazy not be walking with Him all along.

God Bless you Brothers and sisters and I pray my input here will motivate you to seek out the Lord. I pray that this story compels you to give Jesus a try and allow him to give you hope for tomorrow. I was just like you once upon a time and in some cases worse than you. I'm living proof that Jesus forgives.

Repent, then, and turn to God, so that your sins may be wiped out, that times of refreshing may come from the Lord." Acts 3:19

Terence Jeffries; Founder of, City of Refuge Ministries and Outreach Program 40 east Ave Valley Stream, NY 11580

Prison Reentry Resources

New York

Community agencies are available to assist individuals with criminal records find employment.

Center for Employment Opportunities

The Center for Employment Opportunities (CEO) provides rigorous pre-employment training, short-term work crew experience, and long-term job development services to prepare clients with criminal records entering permanent employment. CEO provides services to people with non-violent criminal histories who have completed New York State's Shock Incarceration program or who are on work release, parole, or probation.

Contact:
Center for Employment Opportunities 32 Broadway
New York, NY 10001
212-422-4430
212-422-4855 fax
Web Site: www.ceoworks.org

New York Public Library

The New York Public Library publishes Connections, a directory of organizations in New York City that assist people with criminal records with various services. Connections also includes a guide of necessary information for assisting individuals with criminal records find employment. The guide is regularly updated and can be ordered from the New York Public Library. Some of the information is also available online. Contact:

Correctional Services Librarian
New York Public Library,

Mid-Manhattan Branch 455 Fifth Ave.
New York, NY 10016
212-340-0971
Web Site: www.nypl.org/

The Fortune Society

The Fortune Society is a self-help organization for individuals with
criminal records. Membership extends on a national level. Fortune
offers counseling, referrals to vocational training, job placement,
tutoring in preparation for the High School Equivalency Diploma
(GED), Basic Adult Literacy, English as a Second Language, and
substance abuse treatment. It also offers a wide variety of
alternatives to incarceration services for jail- bound defendants.
Fortune provides discharge planning, case management and
support groups for persons with AIDS or who are HIV positive.

Contact:
The Fortune Society
29-76 Northern Boulevard
Long Island City, NY 11101 212-691-7554
212-255-4948 fax
Web Site: www.fortunesociety.org

Osborne Association

The Osborne Association assists individuals with criminal records,
defendants, people on probation or parole, prisoners and their
families by offering a range of educational, vocational, support and
health services, including defender-based advocacy, day reporting
drug treatment and walk-in harm reduction services, acupuncture
on demand for detox, and intensive AIDS/HIV case management.

Osborne Association
36-31 38th St.
Long Island City, NY 11101 718-707-2600
718-707-3103 fax
E-Mail: info@osborneny.org Web Site: www.osborneny.org

Wildcat Service Corporation

Wildcat provides counseling and work programs for the hard- core
unemployed, especially ex-addicts, individuals with criminal
records, welfare mothers, and out-of-school youth. The three
major work categories are clerical, construction, and maintenance.
Jobs last up to 12 months. Clients must be referred by correctional
programs or legal service providers.

Contact:
Wildcat Service Corporation
17 Battery Place
New York, NY 10004 212-209-6000
Web Site: www.wildcatnyc.org/

STRIVE

Contact:
STRIVE Central
240 East 123rd St., 3rd Floor
New York, NY 10035
212-360-1100
212-360-5634 fax
E-Mail: strivehq@strivecentral.com Web Site:
www.strivenewyork.org/

Exodus Transitional Community

Exodus Transitional Community directly serves recently released
people with criminal records and makes referrals for programs not

offered in-house. Services offered include career counseling, employment workshops including interview techniques, resume writing, job referrals, housing referrals, mental health counseling, substance abuse treatment referral and Alternatives to Violence workshops.

Contact:
Exodus Transitional Community
161 E. 104th St., 4th Floor
New York, NY 10029
917-492-0990; 212-722-6037 development 917-492-8711 fax
E-Mail: exodusdev@aol.com
Web Site: www.etcny.org/

ComALERT

ComALERT is a project of the Office of the District Attorney of Kings County. ComALERT acts in several capacities. One is a service broker, referring clients to various community partners for services such as employment/job development, vocational training; second it monitors the progress of clients in the program; third it acts in a mediation role between probation and social service agencies. It actively works in the community to enhance relationships between the community and the criminal justice system.

Contact:
ComALERT
Office of the District Attorney, King County
350 Jay St.
Brooklyn, NY 11201
718-250-2665
Web Site: www.brooklynda.org/ca/comalert.htm

Developing Justice Project

Developing Justice Project is a project of the Fifth Avenue Committee, a community-based not-for-profit organization that promotes social and economic justice in South Brooklyn, New York. In addition to promoting criminal justice reform, the Developing Justice Project offers walk-in support to individuals with a criminal history. Transitional supportive services in the areas of housing, permanent employment, education and skills development are available through individual case management services.

Contact:
Developing Justice Project
Fifth Avenue Committee
141 Fifth Avenue
Brooklyn, NY 11217
718 237-2017
718 237-5366 fax
E-Mail: fac@fifthave.org
Web Site: http://www.fifthave.org/

Making Career Connections

Making Career Connections is a supported employment program for low or no-income persons, including individuals with criminal histories, who face barriers to employment. Services include barrier assessment and removal, job readiness training (soft skills), job placement assistance and post-employment follow-up.

Contact:
Making Career Connections
278 Clinton Ave.
Albany, NY 12210
518-432-0499
518-432-0826 fax

Good Help Brooklyn

The Brooklyn Chamber of Commerce is a business-driven employment service designed to help Brooklyn businesses and unemployed residents of Brooklyn. The organization works with employers to find job openings, screen potential employees, check references, and follows up with placements.

Contact:
Good Help Program
Brooklyn Chamber of Commerce
25 Elm Place, Suite 200
Brooklyn, NY 11201
718-875-1000
E-Mail: info@brooklynchamber.com
Web Site: www.ibrooklyn.com/site/chamberdirect/goodhelp

Urban Pathways

Urban Pathways provides shelter and support services to homeless men and women in New York. In addition to providing housing programs and services to chemically addicted homeless individuals, Urban Pathways offers the ESTEEM (Employment Skills, Training, Education, Employment, Motivation) program. Services of ESTEEM include vocational and educational opportunities (i.e. counseling, job placement, and GED).

Urban Pathways, Inc.
575 8th Avenue, 9th Fl.
NY, NY 10018
212-736-7385 ext. 29
Web Site: www.urbanpathways.org

Against All Odds

Trying to rebuild your life after spending time in prison can seem like an insurmountable task. What is now being called "Felony Discrimination" subjects many formerly incarcerated individuals to minimal jobs or keeps them out of the work place altogether. Then there are the exceptions to the rule. Meet Randy Kearse, author, speaker, publisher, sales/marketing/promotions extraordinaire. The 13 years, 6 months and 2 days he spent in Federal prison hasn't slowed him down. Since being released 4 years ago he has taken a negative situation and turned it into a positive opportunity.... Now his grind, perseverance, and hustle are the subject of a case study for a program that goes into prisons and teaches entrepreneurship to the inmates...

45 year-old Randy Kearse is a satisfied man. He has authored and published several books, is earning a good living, and is looking forward to his next venture, a newspaper highlighting positive people who have overcome difficult challenges, adversity and are using their lives to enhance the lives of others to be published in the fall. For Kearse, the 13 years he had spent in prison for running a large-scale drug ring is not holding him back; rather, that difficult experience has become the launching pad for his career.

Once deemed a menace to society by a judge who sentenced him to 15 years in prison for conspiracy to distribute narcotics, he served his lengthy sentence (13 years, 6 months and 2 days) and returned to society a changed man. Kearse, a 5 times published author, motivational speaker, and entrepreneur has several stories to tell.

During his incarceration, Kearse thought about how he would earn a living when he was released. He decided writing could be a way to earn some income, which he might later invest in starting a different kind of business, such as a barber shop. Kearse's idea was to write a dictionary of urban language. It was not the first time he tried his hand at writing. At 19 years old, he had written his first book and shared the draft with his girlfriend but she gave him negative feedback and Kearse gave up writing altogether. "I shouldn't have looked to her to validate my work, but I did," he said.

Kearse worked on his book, titled Street Talk: Da Official Guide to Hip-Hop & Urban Slanguage, for six years while incarcerated. At times, he struggled to stay positive. "While I was incarcerated, the people around me kept telling me 'no one's going to read that, you're going back to the streets.' No one encouraged me to pursue positive change. I had to block all of that out. At that point in my life, I was like, 'I don't care what they say.' I used to care a lot about what everyone thought about me, and look what that got me—13 years in prison. At the end of the day, I have to live with me."

A New Way Forward

As soon as Kearse was released, he found a job as a messenger. Although his goal was to publish his book and earn his income from book sales, he knew he needed a reliable income from the messenger job to pay his bills and stay self-sufficient. "You've got to be willing to take a menial job at first," said Kearse. "It's not what you're going to do for your whole life, but you got to start somewhere. You can have a plan, but you need to be flexible because nothing happens exactly how you planned it."

While supporting himself with the messenger job, Kearse looked for an opportunity to publish his book. Rather than presenting an informal manuscript to publishers, Kearse wanted to be able to show them a finished product. One month after his release, he self-published his book through a "print on demand" company. He paid the company a fee to make his book available through online retailers such as Amazon.com. Copies of the book were only printed as they were ordered— there was no inventory —and the company did not edit or promote the book in any way. Recalled Kearse, "I self-published because I wanted to hold the book in my hand and show it to people. I had to believe in what I was doing or no one was going to believe in me. I was bred to do things my way, with no one telling me what to do."

Guerrilla Marketing

With a black-and-white printer his mother gave him, Kearse printed flyers to advertise his book. The flyers displayed the book's cover and a brief summary of its contents, Kearse's contact information, and the website for the on-demand publishing company. "I handed out 500 flyers a day. I distributed them while I was already moving around the city for my messenger job. I gave out *so many* flyers; I would leave them everywhere," he said. Kearse found he could market successfully without spending a lot of money.

You can get the same results on a shoestring budget," he said. "By using a black-and-white printer, I could print more flyers for less money. I printed thousands of flyers off a $90 toner cartridge." Although Kearse did not sell many books initially, his persistent self-promotion resulted in various publicity opportunities, such as requests to interview him for local publications and Internet magazines, as well as invitations to appear on college radio stations.

After several weeks, Kearse read in a newspaper that book publishers would be holding a fair in Manhattan.

He decided to attend the event and try to sell the rights to his book to one of the publishing companies in attendance. "I figured, what's the worst thing that could happen? They'll all say 'no'? I've been shot at, so compared to that, hearing 'no' is nothing. I've experienced too much in my life to be scared of rejection," he said. "So I just walked in there with every intention to sell my book, and when I left, I had an appointment at a publisher's office." Within weeks, the publisher agreed to publish Kearse's book and awarded him a $2,000 advance payment.

Although the book was his passion, the messenger job remained Kearse's priority. Income from his book sales were not high enough to replace a full-time job, and Kearse relied on the messenger position to pay his bills, purchase food, and finance other basic living expenses. After working as a walking messenger for eight months, Kearse had saved enough money, along with the $2,000 book payment, to buy a van. "I saved all the money I could and didn't take on any crazy bills or expenses.

My one goal was to buy that van," said Kearse. "Finally, I was making more money and could start planning for the next level. But I still relied on the messenger job, and treaded lightly on the book thing until it became a reliable source of income. It's a process, but staying focused and taking little steps will lead you to your ultimate goals."

Kearse had started a second book during his incarceration, called *Changin' Your Game Plan: How to Use Incarceration as a Stepping Stone for SUCCESS*. The book offered tools for successfully reentering society after incarceration. After partnering with a publisher on his first book, Kearse had realized that he did not want to share profits with a publishing company (despite the attractive advance the company had paid him). As a result of this experience, Kearse decided to self-publish his second book, using a local print shop instead of the print- on-demand company. In December 2007, Kearse printed 1,000 copies of the book at a local printer for $2500. "I was confident that I had something people were going to buy, so I took them straight to the street myself," explained Kearse. At first, he tried selling the book by setting up a display table in downtown Brooklyn, but he was hesitant to approach people. "Then I started thinking to myself, hold up—something isn't right. You weren't shy when you were selling drugs. How can you be shy doing something that's legal? I just tried to keep the mindset that this is nothing compared to what I used to do," he recalled. Kearse learned that personal connections were the most important driver of sales. "When I was selling drugs and went into a new area, how did I let customers know? I gave out samples to bring people in, then 'boom,' you have your clientele. Just like with selling drugs, you have to get people's attention," he said.

Self-reliance

Eventually, Kearse found he was a natural at selling his books—and, more importantly, selling himself. In early 2008, Kearse was making enough money from book sales to support himself, so he quit his messenger job to focus entirely on promoting and selling his books. He frequently drove his van from city to city to attend book-promotion events (such as book-signings and author expos), which he learned about through Internet and newspaper ads. He explained his strategy at these events: "I don't even put marketing materials on my table. There will be lots of other authors with posters, candy, bookmarks, any gimmick to make a sale. I just cover every inch of my table with my books. It's different, so people noticed. But more important than my setup is me. Most of the authors sit at their table, but I don't sit down at book signings, waiting for people to approach me. People aren't buying my book, they're buying me. People can get what the book is about by reading the back cover in three minutes! So I stand in front of my table, reach out to people, talk to them, engage with them. Half the time when you buy something, the salesman is the one you're really buying, not the product itself." You know, a lot of people, especially from my community, have a gift to be able to use our mouths to sell stuff. We're good salespeople! We just use it in the wrong way sometimes."

In March 2008, Kearse's sales strategy hit a roadblock when he severely damaged his van in a car accident. Having lost his mode of transportation, he began traveling around New York City on foot and public transport, carrying his stock of books and display table by hand. "Losing my van slowed me down tremendously," remarked Kearse. "I tried carrying my whole setup on public transportation for several weeks, but it was too much. So out of desperation—I really needed to make some money—I tried something new." Kearse decided to try selling his books to passengers on the subway. "I put 20 books in a bag and just gave it a try. The first day I sold 13 books, and the second day I sold 12 books. After a couple of weeks, I thought, 'maybe I've really found something here.'"

Kearse settled into a daily routine of selling his books on the subway, focusing on the trains running through Harlem and the South Bronx. He quickly learned that black and Hispanic passengers were most likely to buy from him, and focused on them as his target demographic. He found he was more successful when the train car was not too full; he could connect better with passengers and did not have to yell to be heard. "I never had much pushback from passengers because I'm very courteous. If people aren't feeling what I'm doing, I move on. I'm generally well-received because what I'm doing is positive. I have a positive message."

After refining his sales pitch and his presentation, Kearse found he was able to sell 35 books a day. "I got it down to a science," he said. Kearse caught the ear of a New York Times reporter who was commuting to work on the train. "He watched me do my pitch and liked the way I came across," said Kearse, who took the reporter's business card. "I called him right away to follow up. We spoke a few more times and he pitched the idea of writing a story about me to his editor."

The story, which was printed in July 2010, described Kearse's success and the opening of Kearse's sales pitch: "Excuse me, ladies and gentlemen . . . I am not begging, borrowing or asking for your food. I don't represent the homeless, I'm not selling candy or selling bootleg DVDs. . . I write books."

By the summer of 2010, Kearse had sold 14,000 copies of his books, including his January 2009, title, *From Incarceration 2 Incorporation*, at $10 each. In just four years, Kearse had transformed into a self-made entrepreneur. As he reflected on his success, Kearse felt even more energized about the future.

"Writing and publishing is now my sole profession, but not my end goal," said Kearse in early August 2010. "I'm starting a newspaper soon, which will serve as an advertising vehicle for my books, and I plan to open an international trade company in the next three to five years.

I'm having fun and making money, but I'm not rich. I still have lots of opportunity to grow and expand my experience, and to help other people who have faced some kind of adversity. I now see how much untapped talent there is in prison. It just needs to be channeled in a positive way."

Kearse is also a sought after motivational speaker, using his experiences to educate and empower others on how to succeed against all odds.

Changin' Your Game Plan:
How to use incarceration as a stepping stone for SUCCESS

WORKBOOK – 248 PAGES – 50+ CHAPTERS – Q/A – EXERCISES – $29.99

Changin' Your Game Plan is a practical prison reentry program that helps those currently and formerly incarcerated prepare for the future. The program walks participants through a series of 50 plus soul searching and thought provoking chapters that will help guide them on their journey of change. Along with powerful chapter topics, questions/answers after every chapter, there are exercises that help keep participants further engaged.

Spending more than 30 years of his life incarcerated in one shape, form or fashion, Randy Kearse lived a similar lifestyle as those this program was designed to help. He offers this program as a blueprint to break free of the mindset that keeps people trapped in the revolving door of the criminal justice system.

Changin' Your Game Plan is not based on prison reentry theory or based on a set of thoughtless ideas developed by a nameless official tucked away in a comfortable office who doesn't really understand what the day to day struggles are for someone who is not only getting out of prison physically, but someone who has to break out of the mental prison he/she has been living in (for some most their life).

Order by sending 29.99 Check/Money Order to:
Reentry Strategies 1 W. Prospect Ave #155,
Mt. Vernon, NY 10550

Volume 1 - Randy Kearse

BEYOND
PRISON
PROBATION
AND
PAROLE

REENTRY STRATEGIES LLC

Beyond Prison, Probation & Parole is a motivational film series that features inspiring stories told by formerly incarcerated men and women who have overcome the hurdles, stigmas and challenges associated with returning to society from prison. For many people, getting out of prison can feel like an insurmountable task but there are some who come home and go on to become successful and productive citizens. In Beyond Prison Probation & Parole these individuals not only share their recipes for success, they also tell how they refused to let their past dictate their future. This film series is a low cost, high value approach to reducing the prison recidivism rate by proving success is attainable after incarceration. Each feature in the series uses motivational engagement as a powerful tool to energize, inspire and of course motivate people who want and need to transition from a life of poor choices, substance abuse and criminal behavior, to a positive and productive life.

For more info or purchase: visit www.reentrystrategies.com

Author Afterthoughts

Life out here ain't no picnic. You have to work hard for what you want. You have to be willing to put in the time, exhibit the patience, demonstrate the discipline, use your wisdom, practice your humbleness, appreciate your blessings and most of all take your time.

It's been little over a year and a half since my release from incarceration and I have accomplished a lot. I've had some setbacks, faced some obstacles and I'm still not where I want to be. Every day I strive to do my best, be my best, and give my best. All I came home with was, a plan and a determination to succeed. I'm on the right track and nothing and no one will knock me off this track.

Changin' Your Game Plan, is the key to your successful transition back to society, and maintaining that game plan is the key to your future. Stay focused and diligent!

I went from being a foot messenger to buying my own van and becoming an independent contractor for a courier service. Now I'm starting my own publishing company, Positive Urban Literature Inc. to publish this book. I have many other projects in the pipe line.

The only people who are gonna make it out here are the ones who come home determined to stay out here; The ones who spent their time wisely, the ones who have a plan. There's a lot of opportunity out here. You can take these jewels I've given you and apply them to your life and to your situation or you can discard them. In the end it's your future and what you choose to make of it.

Next year my goal is purchase a piece of real-estate, do some traveling and continue nurturing my plans. Ultimately I plan to start my own Import and Export Company.

Never let your situation get the best of you. Only God and you control your destiny. Since I've come home many people have asked me, what made me change my game plan. What was the single most motivating factor that made me embark on this journey of change...

The answers lie throughout this book, but if I had to sum it all up in a few short words they it would be these...

I did not wanna return to prison! I didn't wanna give the system the power over me ever again! And most importantly, I didn't wanna take my mother through this ever again.

Plain and simple! Peace.
Randy Kearse

Acknowledgement

This book is dedicated to the millions of men and women currently incarcerated who are at a crossroads in their life.

Change isn't easy and I'm not going to pretend that it is. It's a process that will challenge you. Every living thing must change eventually in order to survive. With change comes growth, understanding and empowerment. This book will help you understand you hold the power to change within your own hands.

I thank God for giving me another chance to live my life, for giving me the courage and strength to embrace the journey of change and for the opportunity to share that journey with others. I have to thank my mother Beverly Kearse, my number one supporter and best friend for her unconditional love. My friend from childhood to manhood, Ahmed (A.D) Dickerson for always being there to offer support and encouragement (and for reminding me that I need to pay back that hundred dollars). Jamal Kearse A.k.a Goobie, my big little brother (Thank you for giving me the opportunity to do what I'm doing. Not many people would have done what you did for me without wanting something in return. I love you. Sometimes family is family only until you need them for something). Thank you to all the family and friends who've showed me nothing but love and support. God Bless all of you.

I seen your love ones today.....

I was on the street selling my books and I seen your mother, grandmother, baby momma, your son and your daughter today. I seen your sister, your brother, aunt, uncle, your father. I seen your grandfather, and an old friend you haven't seen in years. It was early in the morning and you could still see the sleep in their eyes. It was late at night and you could see they were tired as hell and they really needed to be in bed gettin' some sleep. It was raining, it was hot as hell, it was cold as an Alaskan winter day, but here they were, standing in line waiting for the bus that would bring them to the city jail, the state prison or the federal penitentiary to visit you.

They were frustrated, angry and hurt by the trials and tribulations of the process they had to endure in order to see you. They dreaded the treatment that they would receive (disrespectful guards, the demeaning search, and waiting process).They dreaded waiting two hours to visit you for 15, 30 minutes or maybe an hour. They dreaded the 5, 6, 7, and 8 hour bus ride upstate. But here they were. Mothers and grandmothers with their withered faces, girlfriends and wives traveling with children too young to understand the journey they were on.

I was there when your love one ran down the bus, missed the bus or was bumped from the bus because it was overbooked. I was there when a love one dang near jumped in front of the bus. I was there when your love one was in tears because they couldn't come see you.

When you wake up today and prepare for that visit, take into consideration the journey that your people were on while you slept in anticipation of seeing them. Think about the sacrifices that your love one has made to be with you today. Whether you're doing 15 days, 15 months, 15 years, or 25 to life, your love ones still come. *I seen your love ones today*